An Archaeology of Town Commons in England

'A very fair field indeed'

An Archaeology of Town Commons in England

'A very fair field indeed'

Mark Bowden, Graham Brown and Nicky Smith

ENGLISH HERITAGE

Published by English Heritage, Isambard House, Kemble Drive, Swindon SN2 2GZ
www.english-heritage.org.uk
English Heritage is the Government's statutory adviser on all aspects of the historic
environment.

The reference numbers for English Heritage images are noted in square brackets in
the captions. The front cover, frontispiece and Figs 1.2, 1.4, 1.5, 1.6, 2.1, 2.2, 2.3, 2.5,
2.6, 2.7, 2.8, 2.9, 3.4, 3.5, 4.1, 4.4, 5.2, 5.5, 6.7, 6.8a, 6.8b, 7.2 and 8.3 are © English
Heritage; p viii and Figs 1.1, 1.3, 3.1, 8.1 and 8.2 are © English Heritage.NMR;
Fig 8.7 is © Crown copyright.NMR; Fig 2.4 is © Crown copyright.NMR (Wingham
Collection); Fig 6.9 is reproduced by permission of English Heritage.NMR; and Figs
3.2, 5.6 and 5.7 are English Heritage (NMR) RAF Photography. Images reproduced by
permission of other bodies have been credited in the acknowledgements and the
relevant captions.

First published 2009

ISBN 978 184802 035 1

Product code 51478

British Library Cataloguing in Publication data
A CIP catalogue record for this book is available from the British Library.

Application for the reproduction of images should be made to the National
Monuments Record. Every effort has been made to trace the copyright holders and
we apologise in advance for any unintentional omissions, which we would be pleased
to correct in any subsequent edition of this book.

The National Monuments Record is the public archive of English Heritage. For more
information, contact NMR Enquiry and Research Services, National Monuments
Record Centre, Kemble Drive, Swindon SN2 2GZ; telephone (01793) 414600.

Typeset in ITC Charter 9.75/13pt

Edited and brought to publication by René Rodgers, Publishing, English Heritage

Indexed by Mark Bowden
Page layout by George Hammond Design

Printed in Great Britain by Norwich Colour Print Ltd.

Front cover: Tewkesbury and the abbey from the Severn Ham. [A0052528]

*Frontispiece: Cattle grazing on Laundress Green, Cambridge, with the River Cam
and Darwin College in the background. [DP046988]*

P viii: Tewkesbury and the Severn Ham in the 1950s–1960s. [AAO91791]

CONTENTS

ACKNOWLEDGEMENTS

The project fieldwork was undertaken by the authors with colleagues in the EH Archaeological Survey and Investigation team, especially Stewart Ainsworth, Wayne Cocroft, David Field, Martin Fletcher, David McOmish, Sarah Newsome, Alastair Oswald, Trevor Pearson and Peter Topping, assisted by John Lord and Mitch Pollington. Aerial photographs were supplied by Damian Grady (Figs 1.1, 1.3, 8.1 and 8.2) and David MacLeod (Fig 3.1), EH Aerial Reconnaissance Officers. Ground photographs were supplied by the authors, Alun Bull (frontispiece and Fig 1.6), Steve Cole (Fig 7.2), James O Davies (front cover), Mike Hesketh-Roberts (Figs 1.5 and 8.3), Derek Kendall (Fig 5.2), Trevor Pearson (Fig 6.8b) and Bob Skingle (Fig 3.4) of the EH Photography, Imaging, Graphics & Survey team. The maps, plans and line drawings for this book were prepared by Deborah Cunliffe (Figs 1.2, 2.1, 2.2, 2.3, 2.5, 2.6, 2.7, 2.8, 2.9, 4.4 and 6.8a); the reconstruction drawings are by Judith Dobie of the EH Archaeological Graphics team (Figs 1.4, 3.5, 4.1, 5.5 and 6.7). Other colleagues in English Heritage have helped considerably with advice and support, notably Ben Cowell, Sarah Green and Jenifer White.

English Heritage would like to thank all those who facilitated our fieldwork and who helped with advice and information during the course of the project, in particular: Graham Bathe, Natural England; James Dinn, Worcester City Council; Dr Henry French, University of Exeter; Mick Jones and colleagues, Lincoln City Council; and Naoual Margoum, DEFRA. We are extremely grateful in particular to Christopher Short of the Countryside & Community Research Institute at the University of Gloucestershire, who showed interest in the project throughout and made many valuable suggestions on a draft of the book. We would also like to thank Mrs Marjorie Bolton and Mrs Irene Lea, who shared with us their first-hand experience of the way of life on urban commons in the early 20th century.

English Heritage is also grateful to the following individuals and institutions: Tony Bartholomew of Tony Bartholomew Photography Ltd (Figs 4.7 and 8.6); Bodleian Library (Fig 6.2); Bristol's Museums, Galleries & Archives (Fig 7.9); Denver Public Library (Fig 7.4); Gloucestershire Archives (Fig 3.7); the Great Torrington Cavaliers (Fig 6.1); Museum of English Rural Life, University of Reading (Fig 6.5); Museum of London (Fig 5.3); The National Archives (Fig 5.9); Andrew Rees of andrewreesphotography.co.uk (Fig 8.4); the Royal Collection (Fig 7.10); John Shakles, Chairman of the John Moore Society, for permission to quote extensively from *Portrait of Elmbury* on p ix; Shrewsbury Museums (Figs 4.2 and 4.6); Mrs J Shuard for freely supplying images from the collection of the late Mr Ron Shuard (Figs 3.8 and 7.1); Adrian Sill, www.donny.co.uk (Fig 7.11); Staffordshire Arts & Museum Service (Fig 7.3); The Tank Museum, Bovington (Fig 5.8); Tewkesbury Borough Council (Fig 3.6); Professor Vanessa Toulmin for freely supplying photographs from the National Fairground Archive (Figs 7.5, 7.6 and 8.5); Tunbridge Wells Museum & Art Gallery (Fig 6.4); and the Virginia Museum of Fine Arts, Richmond (Fig 7.7).

ABBREVIATIONS

EH	English Heritage
NMR	National Monuments Record
RCHME	Royal Commission on the Historical Monuments of England
TNA	The National Archives (formerly the Public Records Office), Kew
VCH	Victoria County Histories

SUMMARY

Historically, towns in England were provided with common lands primarily for grazing the draft animals of those townspeople engaged in trade; they were also used for pasturing farm animals in an economy where the rural and the urban were inextricably mixed and where, in many cases, towns had grown out of or, more usually, been developed upon existing villages. The commoners also had other rights: to collect wood and other materials for building, fuel and crafts; to dig for minerals; and to catch fish in ponds, streams and rivers. Town commons also developed as places of recreation and entertainment, as extensions of domestic and industrial space, and as a locus for military, religious and political activities.

Despite this, however, town commons have been largely disregarded by historians and archaeologists; the few remaining urban commons are under threat and are not adequately protected, even though their wildlife and recreational value has been recognised. In 2002 English Heritage embarked upon a project to study town commons in England, to match its existing initiatives in other aspects of the urban scene. The aim of the project was to investigate the archaeological content and Historic Environment value of urban commons in England and to prompt appropriate conservation strategies for them. The objectives were to research and survey a representative sample of urban com-mons in England, to make available the results of that work in the most appropriate ways to the widest constituency and to promote local community conservation initiatives.

A few of the surviving town commons were surveyed in detail and more cursory work was undertaken in over 50 places. The resulting book is the first overview of the archaeology of town commons – a rich resource because of the relatively benign traditional land use of commons, which preserves the physical evidence of past activities, including prehistoric and Roman remains as well as the traces of common use itself. Crucially, in several cases this reveals how earlier landscape organisation has influenced the layout of present urban space.

The recognition of town commons as a valid historical entity and a valued part of the modern urban environment is a fundamental first step towards successful informed conservation. An important consideration for the future is maintaining the character of town commons as a different sort of urban open space, distinct from parks and public gardens. The fact that they are no longer, generally, working as agricultural commons should not mean that they are treated as urban parks. A local, 'bottom up' approach to the management of these spaces would enable townspeople to enjoy these commons as active participants, developing their interest in both their natural and historical aspects.

'… Elmbury's own field, called the Ham … lay in the triangle between the confluent rivers and the town. It was something of a legal curiosity, and mixed up in its title-deeds were some of the principles of feudalism, capitalism … and communism. The hay crop belonged to a number of private owners, including the squire and the abbey; their boundaries were marked mysteriously by means of little posts. They did not, however, mow their own hay; the Vicar didn't come down from his vestry with a pitching fork; so the hay crop was sold each year, in little parcels none of which by themselves would have been worth the trouble of mowing. It was bid for by groups … who saw to it that they bought contiguous pieces of sufficient area to make a sizeable rick. But while the hay crop was private property, the meadow itself … belonged to 'the burgesses of Elmbury'; these burgesses, the householder, the ironmonger, the draper, the chemist, the doctor, possessed no cows or sheep to graze upon it, so they too each season sold the aftermath by auction and distributed the proceeds, according to an ancient law, among the owners of houses having a frontage on the main street. Nobody got more than a few shillings for his share but at least every man, woman and child in Elmbury had the right to walk and play in the field, which gave them a good possessive feeling about it. It was always 'our Ham'. In winter we shot snipe there, and sometimes hares, without let or hindrance. In the spring … we hunted for plovers' nests and listened to the whistle of the redshanks and the weird sad cry of the curlews which came to the Ham in breeding time. In May, when buttercups gilded it, and the grass was as high as your waist, the courting couples used its cover for their amorous games, flattening out neat circles where they had lain, as if they had rotated on their axis, which perhaps they had, so unquiet alas, is love.

But in June the lovers' hiding places were laid bare, and those same lovers, probably, were toiling and sweating on the wagons, bringing in the hay. Three big rickyards grew up like little towns. Then, while the quick-growing aftermath painted the field green again, and the ochreous sheep or the white-faced Hereford cattle were turned out to graze on it – then the Ham became more than ever Elmbury's playground. Cricket-pitches, on which the ball broke unpredictably, made brown scars on the turf. From the banks of the river jutted out numberless fishing rods …

Meanwhile along the towpath, on summer evenings and Sunday afternoons paraded … shopkeepers and their wives … mothers wheeling their babies out for an airing; boys and girls 'walking out'…

I have devoted rather a lot of space to the Ham because it was part of the life as well as the landscape of Elmbury … It was a very fair field indeed …'

(Moore 1945, 12–14)

Introduction

What are town commons?

A common is an area of land, in private or (increasingly) public ownership, over which rights of common exist. Right of common has been defined as 'a right, which one or more persons may have, to take or use some portion of that which another man's soil naturally produces' (from *Halsbury's Laws of England* (1991), quoted by Clayden 2003, 10). A common field is closed while crops are growing and after harvest thrown open to all the commoners. A common meadow is a common field in which hay is the only crop to be cut. A common pasture is one in which the various proprietors have common rights of pasture. Commons – whether fields, meadows, pastures, marshes, heaths or woods – are common only to the proprietors and to no one else (Kerridge 1992, 1). There are six main rights of common: pasture (the right to graze animals, usually with carefully defined restrictions on the number or type of animals); pannage (the right to feed pigs on fallen acorns and beech mast); estovers (the right to collect small wood for repairs or fuel, furze for fuel, and bracken for animal litter); turbary (the right to cut turf or peat for fuel); piscary (the right to fish in ponds or streams); and common in the soil (the right to take sand, gravel, stone or minerals). Of these, pasture rights are generally regarded as the most significant but the social and economic importance of the other rights and uses should not be underestimated (*see*, for instance, Humphries 1990, 32–4; Neeson 1993, 158–71). Other rights included, for instance, the right to set up tenter frames or to dry laundry (Phillips 1984, 112; Poole 1999, 43). The owner of the common land also has rights: mineral rights; sporting rights; the right to graze animals where the commoners have not occupied all the available 'stints'; the right to plant and cut trees; and the legal rights to grant easements or to maintain action for trespass. However, these owner's rights to minerals, sporting activities and tree planting must not interfere with the commoners' pasturage rights. The general public does not necessarily have any rights at all on commons (Clayden 2003, 10–12, 35, 45).

Despite such authoritative statements as those quoted above, 'common land' poses problems of definition. The complexity of the legal arrangements of different commons leaves areas of doubt: 'It is apparent that the answer to the question "what is common land?" is far from straightforward and there are few definitive answers' (Short 2000, 123). Nevertheless, for the purposes of this study, the definitions put forward by Kerridge and Clayden have been accepted.

Commons are generally thought of as being part of the rural scene. It is the case, however, that most – if not all – historic towns had one or more commons attached to them at some time (and many had arable lands as well, but they are beyond the scope of this study). This was necessary for a number of reasons, not least because the townspeople – most notably those involved in trade – needed pasture for their draft animals; the common was a green precursor to the car park. It was many other things as well: a pastoral and agricultural resource; a place of recreation and entertainment; a source of income for the poor, often in the form of a 'dole'; a source of fuel; a quarry; an extension of domestic and industrial space; and a locus for military and political activities (sometimes subversive). Urban commons could be extensive and occupy a significant proportion of a town's land area; however, they are not always straightforwardly defined. Some (such as Newcastle Town Moor) that are part of the topography of an ancient urban centre are clear enough. However, there is a range of commons that either originated in a rural milieu – and which only later became 'urban' through the promotion of their parent settlement – or that were imposed upon by later new town development. (This is especially true in the case of industrial or spa towns, and seaside resorts, but it also occurred in the case of medieval new towns.) Examples of the former are Godalming, Surrey, a village which did not gain urban status until the 14th century, and Plumstead, Kent, which did not make the transition until the 19th century – their urban commons are rural commons in origin (Lloyd 1992, 74–5; Allen 1997, 64–5). An example of the latter is Brighton, which is largely built over the commons of Brighthelmstone (Girouard 1990, 181–3). Equally, there are commons associated with places that once enjoyed urban status but which have declined, such as Minchinhampton, Gloucestershire, and Corfe, Dorset (Fig 1.1). It is clear, therefore, that the *being* of an urban common is a dynamic, not a static, concept.

Urban status itself is not a readily definable and universally agreed matter. It is widely accepted that the categories of 'rural' and 'urban' were blurred until the Industrial Revolution in England – small towns were often difficult to distinguish from large villages. Criteria of urbanism that are commonly applied include significant concentration of population; specialist economic function; the possession of trading rights; sophisticated political form; complex social structure; and influence beyond the immediate boundaries of the settlement (eg Clark and Slack 1976, 4–5; Beresford 1998, 127–8). Some authorities stress that functions other than the agricultural should predominate (eg Everitt 1974, 29; Laughton and Dyer 1999, 26). An interesting facet of this last criterion is that the requirement to demonstrate that a place did *not* have an agricultural basis in order to qualify as a town tends to make the urban historian underplay, overlook or ignore the town common (and indeed any arable fields belonging to the town). Certainly town commons (like all commons) have been under-studied, despite the pioneering work of Maitland (1897) at Cambridge. A typical text on urban history states in the

Figure 1.1
Aerial view of a small part of Corfe Common showing a Bronze Age round barrow, elements of a prehistoric field system, hollow ways that probably relate to the medieval 'marble' industry, and quarry pits.
[NMR 24139/23]

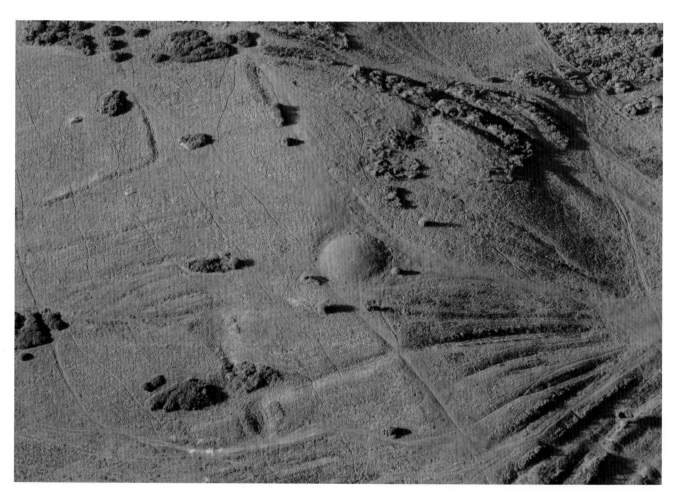

introduction that town commons are an important, or indeed fundamental, part of a town's fabric but fails to mention them again (eg Glennie and Whyte 2000, 173). There are exceptions – the work of Henry French on the commons of Sudbury (2000) and Clitheroe (2003) for instance – but they are rare. (Others have concentrated on enclosure and the end of commons, without considering the commons in their heyday.) For this study we have accepted the general definitions of 'urban' given above and have included places that have at any time in the past qualified as a town.

It is impossible to generalise about the owners and users of urban common rights. Common rights could be vested in all householders in a town or they could be linked to individuals' rights of freedom. Increasingly, they could be restricted to resident freemen or burgesses, or even to senior members of the corporation; financial controls could be introduced to limit access to the wealthier townsfolk. Elsewhere, common rights were vested in burgage properties rather than in individuals. In some places common rights could be shared, conveyed to tenants, leased or sub-let. In some towns different commons could have different rights attached to them (French 2003, 41–2). Not everyone who had common rights exercised them but on the other hand, as a result of leasing (where and when it was allowed) and the use of common lands as a tool for poor relief (Birtles 1999), commons were used by people who had no real rights to them. This complexity lies behind the apparent contradictions noted by John Moore at Tewkesbury in *Portrait of Elmbury* (1945), his fictionalised biography of the town, and which have been articulated in more general terms: 'Common land represents a form of land occupancy that is, at the same time, both traditional and avant-garde' (Short and Winter 1999, 615). As Thompson has noted, it 'was always a problem to explain the commons within capitalist categories. There was something uncomfortable about them. Their very existence prompted questions about the origin of property and about historical title to land' (1991, 159).

Few urban commons survive, being areas peculiarly susceptible to suburban expansion; however, those that do are regarded locally as important places – they are a highly valued recreational resource, a 'green lung' in the city, a haven for wildlife. They are also a reservoir of archaeological remains, though this is rarely recognised. This is true of commons generally – only 3 per cent of the English land surface is common land but 11 per cent of Scheduled Ancient Monuments are on common land (Graham Bathe, *pers comm*). Considerable historical interest attaches to town commons. This book, arising from an English Heritage Research Department project, represents a first attempt to study the archaeology and history of town commons as a category.

The purpose of the English Heritage project

English Heritage's Urban Commons Project was developed because of the identification (by Paul Everson, then Head of Archaeological Survey and Investigation) of urban commons as both an under-studied and an under-protected resource. It was clear that urban commons were almost unexplored by historians and archaeologists – with the exception of Newcastle Town Moor and Minchinhampton Common (*see* pp 11–14, 34, 37 and 81) – and that, while these important urban open spaces are under pressure, they are unprotected because their historic element is not understood:

…we know almost nothing of their use, the types of crops cultivated on them, the kinds of regulations governing them, their economic significance to urban markets, or to individual household budgets. We remain largely ignorant of who used these commons, how they were used, and to what effect, economically and socially.

(French 2000, 176–7)

English Heritage had existing initiatives addressed at urban parks and cemeteries, and at mapping historic urban landscapes more generally (Thomas 2006); however, town commons are a less easily identified sort of urban space. The project sought to establish ways of placing Historic Environment value on urban commons and to highlight that value, responding to the aspirations of *Power of Place* (HERSG 2000).

In 1995 the RCHME had carried out an archaeological survey of Newcastle Town Moor (Lofthouse 1995). This notable public open space, close to the heart of the city, is covered by a complex of earthwork remains of many periods. In 2000–1, while the idea for this project was being developed, the EH Archaeological Survey and Investigation team was

Figure 1.2
Towns and cities mentioned
in the text. The survey
methodology (including
Levels 1, 2 and 3) is
described on p 81.

◇ Level 3 survey

△ Level 2 survey

○ Level 1 survey

● Other town or city
mentioned in the text

undertaking a survey of Minchinhampton Common for the National Trust (Smith 2002). This common retains earthwork remains of all periods from the Neolithic to the Second World War (*see* Fig 2.4). Recent work in completion of the EH-sponsored Urban Archaeology Database for Lincoln, and the development of a research strategy on the basis of it (Jones *et al* 2003), had simultaneously identified the city's South and West Commons as zones of high (but unexplored) potential for revealing the city's history. Both were known to be covered in earthworks – most obviously the remains of cultivation, route ways, quarrying and recreational activity – along with features of miscellaneous and indeterminate type. Neither had been systematically investigated.

The aim of the project was therefore to investigate, through taking a representative sample (Fig 1.2), the archaeological content and Historic Environment value of urban commons in England and to prompt appropriate conservation strategies for them. (The project is described more fully in Chapter 8.)

History of town commons

Origins

The origins of urban commons are obscure. Port Meadow, Oxford, is mentioned in Domesday, but it and many others are certainly of earlier date. Hoskins and Stamp (1963, 12, 130–1) argue that the origins of Port Meadow lie in the early 10th century. Rarely can a foundation date be established: Sudbury's commons were given to the town by Richard de Clare, Earl of Gloucester, in 1262, though here the freemen's use of this land may have pre-dated the gift (French 2000, 177, n38). At Stockport, common rights were 'granted' to the freemen by the lord of the manor in about 1225 (Giles 1950, 73), but again the wording of the grant suggests that this was a formalisation of an existing arrangement. Those commons attached to towns of organic growth may be assumed to have been an integral part of the pre-urban settlement, as at Godalming. This can be reflected in the physical layout of the commons, as at Leicester (French 2000, 174) where the commons originated as the three open fields of the parent settlement. 'New' towns have more tightly drawn boundaries and therefore, apparently, little common land,

though (as noted above) many of them, such as Petersfield (Hoskins and Stamp 1963, 5, 40), were laid out over existing commons (Fig 1.3). Despite this apparent paucity of knowledge, historical, place-name and archaeological evidence may be brought together to suggest some themes in the origin of urban commons (this is discussed further in Chapter 2).

Figure 1.3
Aerial photograph of the surviving part of Petersfield Heath Common to the south-east of the town.
[NMR 23309/02]

Status and use

Commons are now private property. In their report, Hoskins and Stamp stated that all common land 'belongs to someone, whether an individual or corporation, and has done so from time immemorial' (1963, 4). The latter part of this statement has been challenged because, it is argued, the idea of property rights has evolved from feudal custom which emphasised reciprocal obligations rather than property as such (Short and Winter 1999, 616 and references therein). Nevertheless, what distinguishes common from other land is the existence of 'rights of common' held by individuals or groups other than the owner (*see* pp 20, 23–4 and 33–9).

Urban commons are infrequently mentioned in medieval records and, aside from rare instances, their presence is only revealed when they are subject to dispute, as in Coventry where in 1480 Laurence Saunders challenged the right of powerful men in the borough to overstock the commons with sheep (Platt 1976, 122). This was one of a number of such disputes, frequently leading to riots, over Coventry's commons during the 15th century (Thompson 1991, 122–3). The historical record for the post-medieval period is greater but still has many gaps and has not been studied in depth, with the almost unique exceptions of

Sudbury and Clitheroe (French 2000; 2003). These studies concentrate on what is perceived as the primary *raison d'être* of urban commons – grazing. There has been as yet almost no historical study of other organised activities on urban commons and few on the unorganised ones; an exception is Poole's study of civil unrest on Bristol's commons (1999).

More widely, commons have been central to recent historical debate about social relations and production in the post-medieval period (briefly summarised by Short and Winter 1999, 615). However, this debate has not specifically embraced the urban common. Humphries, for instance, has argued convincingly for the economic and social importance of keeping a cow on common land for a family otherwise dependant on low agricultural wages and for the importance to the poor of the 'despised' other fruits of the rural commons – literally fruits but also wildlife and herbs, fuel, stone and gravel, brushwood and other raw materials for handicrafts (1990, 21–35; Fig 1.4). This must be as true for urban commons as it is for rural ones. Some commentators have accepted the statements of contemporaries that the urban commons were 'of little use' to the inhabitants (eg Giles 1950, 81–4), but the voices of the poorer inhabitants are largely missing and the fact that they attempted to oppose enclosure, albeit almost invariably without success, suggests that they did perceive a use and a value in the commons (*see* Neeson 1993). One example of successful resistance to enclosure occurred at Berkhamsted in the 17th century where, in a remarkable prelude to the better known fence breaking of 1866, illegal fences placed by the Duchy of Cornwall were repeatedly broken down and the common remained open (Eversley 1910, 49–51). In some places the non-pasture rights came to the fore and significant industries developed on the commons – for instance gun flint manufacture at Brandon (Pearson 1996), turnery at Wymondham and Berkhamsted, and chair-making at Chesham (Everitt 2000, 232–3). Commons were also important places for nomadic workers.

Henry French has identified five types of urban common in early modern England (2000, 173–6):

i) grazing rights exercised by freemen over land, often in private ownership, within or adjoining the town and usually restricted to certain times of the agricultural year;

Figure 1.4
'Fruits of the common.' With the development of the 'food for free' movement (Mabey 2001) and the resurgence of interest in local foods, such garnering may again become a significant activity on urban commons.

ii) lowland arable, usually in unenclosed strips, owned by the manorial lord(s) or corporation, access to which was theoretically restricted but in practice sometimes, and increasingly, extended to all ratepayers;

iii) land within the town owned by the manorial lord(s) or corporation, with post-harvest and fallow grazing rights on the arable, and dedicated pasture, meadow and waste;

iv) similar to iii, the 'inland' commons of upland towns within the boundaries of the settlement consisting of arable (usually in strips) and pasture, which was linked to

v) upland grazing rights of town residents and inhabitants of neighbouring townships over surrounding moorland (including greens and verges), available for summer grazing and as a source of fuel and game.

French (*pers comm*) has also identified four broad geographical zones of urban commons:

i) The North-West, where small market towns retained their commons into the 19th century;

ii) The Pennine belt, with industrialising towns that could include vast commons extending into neighbouring parishes; enclosure acts in such towns disaggregated common rights – possibly a deliberate attempt by the town authorities to uncouple themselves from their rural origins;

iii) The Central belt, corresponding to the classic midland open field agriculture area – mostly consisting of old shire boroughs (some well outside the actual region, eg Newcastle upon Tyne); these were historically significant towns with commons; and

iv) Southern England: a less well-defined area, but mainly consisting of small boroughs and non-corporate towns, declining in the 18th century, or at least lacking in dynamism.

The current archaeological evidence is not at variance with this broad picture. For instance, town commons have been difficult to identify on the ground at all in much of south-western England, possibly reflecting a different approach to land use on the urban periphery in this area. However, the archaeological evidence does emphasise two different aspects of urban commons. The first is the wide range of activities undertaken on the commons (discussed further below); the second is the dynamism of common use, suggesting that the categories outlined by French for the early modern period may have been subject to considerable change over the centuries.

Even within the early modern period, the historical record suggests change at various levels. Agricultural activities on urban commons were regulated by custom but, as French notes, 'custom was not immutable' (2000, 178). Rules had to be changed from time to time, in order to deal with increased stocking, infringements or other issues. (As noted above, there appear to have been no studies of how other activities – such as quarrying, fuel gathering or tentering – were regulated.) The use of commons could change due to external economic and social factors, as well, such as the changing fortunes or demographic profile of the town, or rising population. Disputes were frequent – over individual cases and over more fundamental matters of governance – and often ended in the law courts; even where cases were unsuccessfully prosecuted they could lead to changes in common management. Nor was the extent of commons static. Overstocking was a frequent, and generally increasing, problem but at some times and in some places town commons were underused. Therefore urban commons might be, and often were, enclosed; they could suffer encroachment and alienation. On the other hand more land was sometimes purchased as overstocking became a problem, so urban commons could grow as well as shrink. Space on commons could also be appropriated for public buildings that the community felt needed to be hidden or isolated, such as the prison at Stockport (Giles 1950, 86) or infectious disease hospitals, as at Lincoln (Brown 2003, 12).

Recreation in various guises is an under-recorded aspect of the use of urban commons but it is one which is clearly important. Horse racing is attested on many commons as are cricket, football, golf and other ball games. Archaeological evidence for these activities, and less attractive ones such as bear-baiting, can still be seen. Fairs and festivals survive on many urban commons to this day, as at Newcastle upon Tyne, Lincoln and Great Torrington, for instance. It was often the more personal unorganised pursuits, such as those noted by John Moore (*see* p ix), that were most valued by the townspeople; however, this value was rarely acknowledged by those who wished to enclose and appropriate the commons.

Urban commons could also become associated with radicalism and political unrest through repeated use for meetings and rallies – as in the case of Brandon Hill, Bristol (Poole 1999) – or through one tragic event such as the Peterloo Massacre in Manchester (though it is unclear whether St Peter's Field was common ground). It may not be an entirely unrelated matter that commons were also frequently the scene of military gatherings and parades.

Enclosure and decline

Loss of common land generally to the enclosure movement between the 16th and 19th centuries was dramatic, particularly in the well-populated south and east of the country where the pressure for agricultural 'improvement' was greatest (Short and Winter 1999, 616–17) – this affected urban as well as rural commons. However, the virtual disappearance of urban commons has had many other, sometimes more pressing, causes such as decline in grazing; exhaustion of mineral resources; pressure of housing and other development; replacement of draft animals with mechanised transport; availability of cheap coal; and a desire to 'tidy up' and regulate public open space. Urban commons have been enclosed and either built over or turned into parks, municipal gardens and cemeteries. Enclosure could begin at an early date; Stockport's commons began to be enclosed around or soon after 1300, less than a century after they were 'granted' (Giles 1950, 73). Part of Chichester's common seems to have been appropriated by the king and given to the bishop in 1229 (Munby 1984, 324). In the post-medieval period demand for building space, for both industrial and domestic purposes, was one of the chief drivers of urban common enclosure movements (Carter 1983, 139). Examples of this include Bolton, East Retford, Macclesfield, Stockport (Giles 1950, 92) and, most notoriously, Nottingham.

Nottingham, unable to expand because it was almost surrounded by urban commons that the freemen and burgesses had consistently defended against enclosure and development, became seriously congested as it prospered and grew. (At Stamford it was the ownership of the town by an individual – the lord of the manor – that prevented the development of building over the common fields (Hoskins 1988, 229).)

Only after the Reform Act of 1832 (widely known as the Great Reform Act) and the replacement of the Charter Corporation by a Borough Council was it possible to obtain an Enclosure Act in Nottingham in 1845. The act appointed three commissioners to apportion allotments and to lay out a street system. Their road plan followed the old paths across the commons so that the street plan of much of Nottingham today reflects the form of the commons. However, the new owners, of which there were more than 400, began development work before the overall plan was finalised and laid out their plots without reference to the plan or to any of their neighbours (Carter 1983, 140).

At Dewsbury there was a variation on this theme. The influx of immigrant workers for the woollen trade led to the erection of squatters' dwellings on the town's commons. Enclosure was sought in order to control this haphazard development (Broadbent 1997, 209). Squatting was an issue on other urban commons, such as Warminster.

In the case of Nottingham, the commons had been retained almost in their entirety for so long due to the strength of the interested parties – property owners who feared that their slum rents would fall if the commons were enclosed and housing development took place. Elsewhere, however, as in the rural milieu, the enclosure of urban commons was undertaken largely for the benefit of the prosperous and powerful at the expense of the poorer members of society. Even where an enclosure scheme had ostensibly disinterested and public-spirited intentions, the results could be dubious, as in the murky case of Stockport's 1805 Enclosure Act. The proceeds of enclosing Stockport's remaining common lands were supposed to be used to build and endow a poorhouse and to relieve the Poor Rate (to the benefit mainly of small cottage occupiers). However, although the poorhouse was built by the raising of a £1,000 mortgage, the remainder of the sum raised by the sale of plots of common, in excess of £7,000, disappeared. Despite several demands, no proper enquiry was ever made (Giles 1950, 92–104) and it has to be presumed that some of the commissioners and other interested parties stole the money.

As well as the loss of the economic benefits of common land through enclosure, in many cases the working classes and poorer inhabitants also lost access to open space for recreation. In some places this was mitigated by the deliberate laying out of parks and walks for public recreation, an idea which had its origins in the 17th century (*see*, for instance, Elliott 2000, 145); however, the activities that could take place in such spaces were limited to the sedate and the polite. As Borsay (1986, 131) notes, formal walks 'were decidedly in the fashionable camp and helped forge among the promenaders those cultural bonds of refined behaviour that welded together élite society, and separated them from the perceived barbarism of plebeian life'. (In the 19th century, however, walks were created in Lincoln to 'keep the city's men out of public houses and in the open air with their families' (Lincoln Reference Library: Abell Collection, *Agriculture & Commons* 1, 84b).) Manicured 'walks' were a means by which, through the 18th century, 'an increasingly urbanized society sought to retain contact with a retreating rural world' (Borsay 1986, 132) but, ironically, this was happening at the same time as the towns were shedding their most intimate genuine connections with rural life by enclosing their commons. In fact, where polite walks replaced areas of common – as at Maidstone, Northampton and Shrewsbury – they were actively driving out the rural. In Sheffield more than 7,000 acres of commons were enclosed between 1779 and 1810 'without one rod, pole or perch being set aside for purposes of public recreation' (Hammond 1931, 258–9). The enclosure of Crooks Moor 'gave a death blow' to the horse racing that traditionally took place there, while the Assembly Green at Brightside, which had been a place for sports and pastimes for the townspeople, was handed over to the lord of the manor (ibid). Giles (1950, 105) has argued that in Stockport the loss of recreation space was negligible because the recorded 18th-century recreations on the commons had died out before 1785 and that at the time of the final enclosures in the early 19th century every part of the town was within 15 minutes' walk of open country. This ignores the possibility that *unrecorded* leisure activities (of the sort remembered by John Moore (*see* p ix) in Tewkesbury) may have continued and that (again to refer to Moore) the people had no sense of 'ownership' and no rights over the countryside, no matter how adjacent. Similarly, Joseph Gutteridge regretted the loss of Coventry's commons in the mid-19th century, remembering them as a 'veritable paradise' where he had been able to roam 'without let or hindrance' (quoted in

Thompson 1991, 123–4). It was the potential loss of recreation space that led to the foundation of the Commons Preservation Society in 1865. The society was animated by two ideas: 'one, that the people of this country should have some interest in the land of the country, the other, that the amenities of everyday life should be placed within reach of rich and poor alike' (Eversley 1910, vii).

Many historians assume that the enclosure of town commons was 'a good thing'. Clark mentions the enclosure of Gloucester's commons in 1797 in passing, as one of a list of successful reform measures, without any discussion (1984, 335). Others (eg Thompson 1991, chapter 3) have persuasively argued the opposite view. However, despite the hardships that enclosure undoubtedly brought upon the poorer members of the urban community, the enclosure and alienation of urban commons was, arguably, inevitable. In the face of decline in the demand for an agricultural resource within towns and the increasing pressure of rapidly expanding urban populations there was perhaps, in many cases, little that the authorities could do but enclose. A more equitable division of the proceeds of enclosure could have been made, however, in every case. Enclosure was always controversial, as a number of studies have shown (eg Neeson 1993; Archer 2000, 245–6) and sometimes led to direct action and civil unrest, as it famously did at Berkhamsted in 1619 and 1866 (Eversley 1910, 42–54; Cowell 2002), at Sheffield, where in 1791 rioting was met by military action (Hammond 1931, 260–2), and elsewhere (see Allen 1997).

Figure 1.5
Hocktide or 'Tutti Day',
Hungerford, 20 April 2004.
At the Hocktide Court the
common officials are elected
for the coming year.
[NMR DP000546]

Figure 1.6
Cattle on Scholars' Piece,
Cambridge, with King's
College in the background.
[NMR DP046986]

Protest against enclosure was, to some extent, more successful in towns than in villages (Thompson 1991, 121–6) but it only tended to delay, rather than prevent, enclosure. Even the resourceful inhabitants of Pockthorpe, Norwich, ultimately lost their battle for Mouse-hold Heath (*see* Clark 1990). However, while 18th-century riots, and more peaceable protests as at Atherstone (Thompson 1991 152–8; Neeson 1993, 79, 274), had little effect on the process of enclosure, by the later 19th century the tide was turning and Berkhamsted Common was one of a string of successes for the Commons Preservation Society (Eversley 1910).

Few commons now survive – even partly – as an element of the urban scene. Nevertheless, where they do survive (often adjacent to what are now small towns) there may still be traditional ceremonies associated with them – as at Hungerford (Fig 1.5) and Stockbridge – and elements of traditional use, particularly in the case of grazing; horses and cattle can still be seen on the urban commons of England (Fig 1.6).

2

The land before the commons

Ancient landscapes preserved

While the main thrust of this work is on the archaeology of urban commons as such, an important secondary consideration has been the earlier landscape history of these areas and the extent to which the relatively benign land use of commons has led to the preservation of the remains of earlier periods. These remains are, anyway, directly relevant to the history of the commons; in some cases they have a bearing on the origins of the commons and certainly formed significant landmarks within them.

Prehistoric

The most obvious prehistoric features preserved on urban commons are burial mounds, such as those seen at Beverley and Oxford; however, there are other, more fugitive, remains. The most extensive are the field systems, linear ditches and related features seen at Beverley, Biggleswade, Hungerford and elsewhere; perhaps the most surprising are the earthworks of a possible late prehistoric settlement enclosure on Newcastle Town Moor, within a mile and a half of the busy city centre.

Barrows

Minchinhampton Common boasts what is perhaps the earliest surviving earthwork on an urban common, the probable Neolithic burial mound known as Whitfield's Tump (Smith 2002, 13–14; Fig 2.1). But there are also early Bronze Age barrow cemeteries at Corfe and Petersfield as well as Oxford. The 'Round Hill' on Port Meadow, Oxford, is in fact something of a cheat as the earthwork now visible is the result of excavation of the site in the mid-19th century (Lambrick and McDonald 1985, 95). However, the genuine Bronze Age barrow which lies beneath it did survive to be recognised by antiquarians. It is one member of a large cemetery, the other mounds having been destroyed at some unknown time. The mechanism of their destruction is also unknown, as ploughing – the usual culprit – is presumably not the agent here.

The barrows on Corfe Common are part of an extensive linear cemetery that continues along the ridge to the east. Eight well-preserved mounds survive on the common, occupying high points and forming prominent landmarks (Fletcher 2003, 8–9, 15; *see* Fig 1.1). There are no recorded ring ditches in the area surrounding Corfe Common, so this cemetery seems to have survived in its entirety. At Petersfield Heath Common (*see* Fig 1.3) there is a cemetery of 21 barrows, at least 5 of them large round barrows on the eastern side of the heath, standing up to 2m high and generally in good condition. One or two barrow mounds appear to have been lost to the landscaping of the golf course (NMR: SU 72 SE 18). Again, there are no recorded ring ditches in the immediate area, so this may be a more-or-less

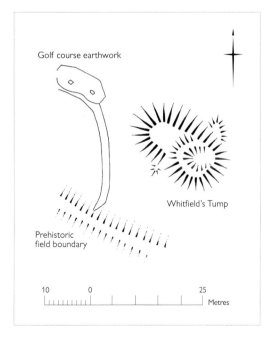

Golf course earthwork

Whitfield's Tump

Prehistoric field boundary

10   0   25
Metres

Figure 2.1
Whitfield's Tump, Minchinhampton Common, a badly mutilated Neolithic long barrow. The prehistoric field bank to the south is a later, possibly Bronze Age or Iron Age, boundary.

Figure 2.2
Iron Age square barrows
(labelled 6–12) surviving as
earthworks on Westwood
Common, Beverley, amongst
later landscape features.
There is a further group of
barrows surviving to the
north-east.

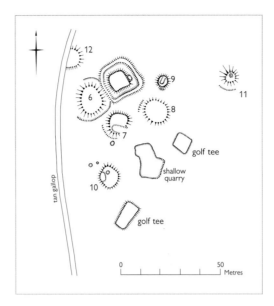

Figure 2.3 (opposite, top)
Plan of Hungerford showing
the alignment of the
medieval common and town
on the prehistoric or Roman
field system (after Astill
1978, fig 11 and Newsome
2005, fig 7). Later features
on the common – which
include cultivation remains,
tree-planting rings, quarries
and 20th-century military
installations – have been
omitted.

Figure 2.4 (opposite, bottom)
Aerial photograph of
Minchinhampton Common
in 1959 showing part of The
Bulwarks; also visible are
medieval or early post-
medieval pillow mounds in
the foreground overlying an
earlier earthwork connected
to The Bulwarks, along with
quarries and the earthworks
of the golf course.
[HAW 9391/15, 31 May
1959]

intact cemetery. Nevertheless, it lies within a geologically defined zone in which there are numerous barrow cemeteries and also numerous commons. This will be discussed further on p 19.

Several of the barrows on Westwood Common, Beverley, are of Iron Age origin and very rare – the current survey has added two previously unrecorded examples (Pearson and Pollington 2004, 15–18, 48). Even more rare is their survival as earthworks (Fig 2.2); the vast majority of Iron Age square barrows are known only from cropmarks on aerial photographs. Their survival must be due to the later status of their surroundings as uncultivated common land.

Fields and linear ditches

Though Port Meadow's extensive archaeological remains – other than 'Round Hill' – were first found by aerial photography only in the 1930s, many of them were subsequently discovered to be surviving as very slight earthworks by R J C Atkinson. Surveys and excavations revealed the existence of further Bronze Age barrows and Iron Age settlements. More aerial survey, fieldwork and excavation in the latter part of the 20th century identified five distinct phases of activity leaving visible traces on Port Meadow, either as earthworks or differential vegetation. Two of those phases were prehistoric, confirming and building upon the earlier findings. There were at least six Bronze Age round barrows and three groups of middle Iron Age farmsteads accompanied by ditched paddocks. Environmental archaeology suggests a higher

water table in the Iron Age than in the earlier period and also provides evidence that the area was principally under pasture and supported similar grassland communities to those which exist on Port Meadow today. In addition, however, there was evidence for plants of disturbed ground, characteristic of rural settlements and farmyards that are not now represented on the meadow. The farmsteads may represent consecutive rather than simultaneous settlement and, given the evidence for winter waterlogging, may have been seasonally occupied for summer grazing. These Iron Age settlements on Port Meadow are 'unrivalled in extent and quality of preservation' in the upper Thames valley (Lambrick and McDonald 1985, 100).

Field systems with either certain or possible prehistoric origins have also been identified at Beverley, Corfe, Doncaster, Hungerford and Minchinhampton. At Hungerford the low banks defining the fields were first identified by ground observation, though aerial photography subsequently revealed further details (Newsome 2005). The fields are aligned west–north-west to east–south-east and are morphologically similar to prehistoric and Roman fields on the Berkshire and Marlborough Downs (Bowden *et al* 1993; McOmish 2005). Importantly, it was noted that at least one existing field boundary to the south of Hungerford Common appears to be lying on one of the prehistoric field boundaries (Newsome 2005, 14); in fact the general alignment of the common, and the medieval part of the town itself, seems to be respecting the prehistoric field system (Fig 2.3). The plan of the town (east of High Street at least) and its common, laid out some time between 1170 and 1296 (Astill 1978, 29), was dictated by the visible remains of the prehistoric fields, though the open fields of an earlier medieval village settlement may also have had an influence on the western half of the town (ibid, 30). The groups of burgage plots between High Street and Back Lane on the east can be read as occupying a series of rectangular prehistoric or Romano-British fields.

Linear ditches of various forms, and probably of different dates, are found on several commons. At Minchinhampton, The Bulwarks offer a particularly enigmatic glimpse of past land use (Fig 2.4). They comprise a substantial bank and ditch, the overall height being – in places – over 2m, cutting off the eastern side of the common (nearest the town) in an irregular curve which includes two unexplained abrupt angles. The Bulwarks appear to encircle the town but the ditch is on the 'inside', so they are not a defensive work. There are numerous gaps but all appear to be later breaches. Nearer the town some sections have been completely or nearly levelled. The date of The Bulwarks is entirely unknown. Excavations in the 1930s recovered late Iron Age, Roman and earlier artefacts, leading to the suggestion that The Bulwarks represent a late Iron Age 'oppidum' (Clifford 1937, 297). This is somewhat controversial, not least because little other evidence for activity of this date has ever been recovered from Minchinhampton – 'oppida' are, almost by definition, wealthy places with much material culture. Before the 1930s excavations Crawford (1925) had suggested a medieval date for The Bulwarks. This explanation has recently been revived and Darvill has suggested that The Bulwarks are a wood bank, separating woodland from the fields of Minchinhampton (1998, 15). Alternatively they could be a deer park pale or an early medieval estate boundary (Smith 2002, 23–4). Another similar earthwork on Minchinhampton Common is the Amberley Cross Bank – an isolated length of bank and ditch on a slightly curving line (ibid, 24–5); excavations recovered artefacts of similar date (Clifford 1937, 293) to those in The Bulwarks. The most likely explanation for the Amberley Cross Bank is that it is an unfinished work and this might be the best clue to The Bulwarks as well – that they represent a failed or unfinished 'oppidum', explaining the comparative lack of rich contemporary finds in the area.

Berkhamsted Common is also distinguished by a surviving linear ditch – traditionally part of the Chiltern Grim's Ditch. Gaps in this apparently 25-mile-long boundary have been explained as the result of the builders encountering dense woodland on clay. Leaving aside the inherent flimsiness of this explanation, it might appear at Berkhamsted that the survival of the Chiltern Grim's Ditch as an earthwork is due to the common – the ditch ends abruptly at either side, where it has perhaps been levelled by the normal operations of agriculture. However, an alternative view is that the Chiltern Grim's Ditch is an agglomeration of features of different dates and functions, and that the supposed section of the ditch on Berkhamsted Common is either a cross-ridge dyke, possibly of late Iron Age date (Thompson and Bryant

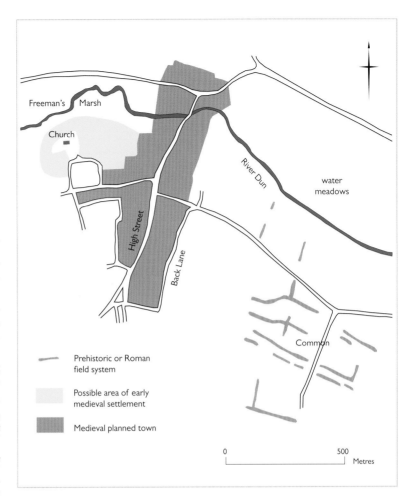

Freeman's Marsh

Church

River Dun

water meadows

High Street

Back Lane

Common

— Prehistoric or Roman field system

Possible area of early medieval settlement

Medieval planned town

0   500
                Metres

2005, 3) that survives almost in its entirety, or part of an early medieval deer park boundary (Dyer 1963, 47); in the latter case, the argument about its survival on the common stands. Thompson and Bryant (2005, 3) suggest that further earthworks, perhaps contemporary with the linear ditch, survive on Berkhamsted Common and on the neighbouring Ashridge Estate; however, these were not examined during the current project.

Linear features on Westwood Common, Beverley, are interpreted as hollow ways but at least one changes direction, suggesting that it may follow a pre-existing feature, possibly an earlier boundary earthwork (Pearson and Pollington 2004, 32–4).

It will be clear from the above that linear earthworks, in many instances, are neither well dated nor well understood.

Settlement

Prehistoric settlement on Port Meadow has already been mentioned. However, this survives only as subsurface remains giving rise to cropmarks. On Newcastle Town Moor there are the remains of two possible prehistoric settlement enclosures, one of them surviving as upstanding, albeit slight, earthworks (Fig 2.5; *see also* Fig 4.4). This small circular earthwork enclosure, measuring about 32m in diameter, lies on the eastward-facing slope of Race Hill; it is defined on its upslope side by a low bank, up to 0.3m high, with an external ditch only 0.2m deep. The downslope side is defined by a scarp about 0.4m high. A flattened

area on the east side may show the position of an entrance. Internal features are slight, the most obvious being a small mound with a hollow at its centre; this is possibly a later mine shaft head, rather than anything to do with the enclosure. The enclosure has been damaged by digging on the south-west side and by drainage ditches associated with surrounding ridge-and-furrow. The shape and form of the enclosure suggests that it is a small late prehistoric enclosed settlement though demonstrable proof of this interpretation is lacking. The other possible settlement on Newcastle Town Moor was discovered in unusual circumstances when regrading of an area of opencast mining around Race Hill revealed the soil mark of a rectangular ditched enclosure on the summit (*see* Fig 4.4). The enclosure measures 50m east to west by 65m transversely and has a single entrance, approximately 10m wide, on the east side, the ditch on either side ending in a flared terminal. The south-east corner of the enclosure is unclear and the ditch narrows on the west side. This could be the remains of a late prehistoric or Romano-British enclosure; it is similar to known settlements of this date in the region in terms of its size, shape, topographical location and east-facing entrance (Lofthouse 1995, 49–50).

Another possible prehistoric enclosure is represented by an earthwork on The Hoad, a substantial isolated hill that forms part of the common lands of Ulverston. This is a larger, oval enclosure, up to 150m long and 50–60m wide (Elsworth 2005a, 57).

Landscapes

The individual monument types described above can be viewed together, where possible, to reveal entire landscapes. Biggleswade Common retains surviving earthworks of round barrows, probably of Bronze Age date, a trackway, field system and settlement enclosures; the latter might date to the later Bronze Age, the Iron Age or the Romano-British period. There is also a possible Roman villa or temple complex (*see* Fig 8.7). Cropmarks in arable fields adjacent to the common show that these are the surviving upstanding elements of a wider prehistoric landscape, preserved through common usage from the medieval period onwards. Ironically, however, while the cropmarks have been noted on aerial photographs and recorded, the earthworks surviving on the common had largely been overlooked until this

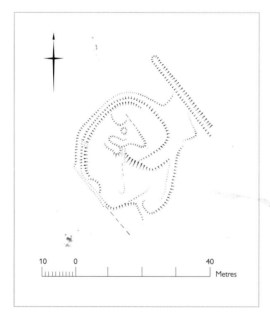

Figure 2.5
Earthworks of a possible prehistoric enclosure on Newcastle Town Moor. To the north-east is one of the side ditches of the 18th-century racecourse. To the south-west the enclosure has been truncated by narrow ridge-and-furrow. Near the centre of the enclosure is the top of a mine shaft (see also Fig 4.4).

10   0   40
Metres

project took place. Parts of the common also reveal ridge-and-furrow and medieval or later earthwork enclosures, as well as more recent remains.

Roman

The ability of commons to preserve the remains of earlier periods is perfectly illustrated by the case of the Roman camps at Bootham Stray (Fig 2.6), 2.5km north of the legionary fortress at York (Welfare and Swan 1995, 135–6). Here 18th-century records suggest the existence of as many as eight Roman camps; two are now recognisable. The only surveyable earthworks are in the southern part of Camp 1, which lies on Bootham Stray; its northern part – lying within the 'half-year lands' (common land grazed for half the year and arable for the remainder) bordering the common – is visible only as parchmarks on aerial photographs. Camp 2, also lying within the 'half-year lands' to the west, survives as an earthwork but is so slight as to be deemed impossible to survey in the 1990s. Bootham Stray, used for permanent pasture, has retained what the 'half-year lands', ploughed occasionally (and showing traces of straight, narrow ridge-and-furrow), have not. However, the survival of these Roman earth-works even upon the common is fortuitous since most of Bootham Stray was put under the plough during the mid-20th century.

More extensive, though less obvious, Roman remains are found on the South Common at Lincoln. Intrusive activities in the 19th and 20th centuries led to the discovery of various Roman finds, including fragments of a military tombstone and cremations, presumably from a roadside cemetery. It has long been known that Ermine Street crossed South Common but its route was unknown. The new survey has shown that the road survives in part, with a short stretch of visible agger, but that more of its route is indicated by a linear arrangement of small quarries, markedly different from those elsewhere on the common and defining a zone not more than 60m wide. These presumably represent robbing of road materials. Part of the eastern boundary of South Common is defined by the road (Field 2005, 14–17, 28–31; Fig 2.7). At right angles to Ermine Street a series of slight linear scarps can be identified. In one case a right-angled corner indicates that these might have formed small square or rectangular plots. Similar features on the same alignment at greater distances from the road (and as far east

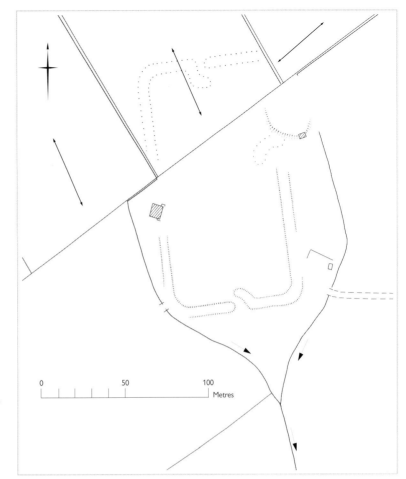

as Canwick Park) suggest that this is an exten-sive field system, rather than just roadside enclosures. Interestingly the boundary of the medieval hospital, The Malandry, shares the alignment (ibid, 32–3). The implication is that South Common preserves not only the remains of a major Roman road but also a contemporary field system, the alignment of which, as at Hungerford, continued to have significance into the medieval period.

Early medieval

Earthworks of early medieval (5th–10th century) date are everywhere rare and urban commons are no exception. The possibility that the Chiltern Grim's Ditch on Berkhamsted Common is an early medieval deer park pale has been mentioned above but firm evidence to support the idea is lacking.

An oval earthwork enclosure (Fig 2.8) on Beverley's Westwood Common offers another possibility, here with some evidence. Lying on the west side of the common the enclosure stretches from the crest of the Newbald Valley

Figure 2.6
Remains of Roman Camp 1 on Bootham Stray, York; the double-ended arrows represent the direction of ploughing of the 'half-year lands'.
[After Welfare and Swan 1995, fig 112]

15

Roman road

Features laid off
from Roman road

19th- and 20th-century
military features

100   0   500

Metres

Figure 2.7
Ermine Street crossing
South Common, Lincoln.
The line of the Roman road
is marked partly by a short
stretch of surviving agger,
but mainly by distinctive
quarries. Plot boundaries,
which seem to take their
alignment from the Roman
road are also marked, as are
19th- and 20th-century
military features.

for 220m to the south side of a spur of higher ground rising from the valley floor. It is 140m wide and the surrounding earthwork is slight, except on the north side of the valley where the bank is up to 1m high. Two later hollow ways following the bank at this point have before been erroneously interpreted as substantial external ditches. There are gaps in the perimeter but those on the north-west side appear to be later breaches. The original entrance was probably to the east, where there is a 20m-wide gap in the perimeter earthworks, giving access

along the level floor of the valley. The south-western side of the enclosure now forms the boundary of the common. There are no visible internal features but it is possible that a spring arose within or adjacent to the enclosure. This enclosure has no defensive strength, either from its position or from its surrounding bank and ditch. It may have been a settlement or perhaps a stock enclosure. It has been recorded previously as a Romano-British settlement. Two pieces of earthwork evidence give clues to its date. Firstly, the common boundary on the south-west changes alignment abruptly where it meets the west and south sides of the enclosure, indicating that the enclosure was in existence when the common was established and that the boundary was deliberately laid out so as to incorporate the enclosure – Westwood Common was certainly in existence by the 13th century. Secondly, the enclosure overlies a field system of probable late prehistoric or Romano-British date and therefore it is probably of late Romano-British or early medieval date. The deliberate inclusion of the enclosure within the common may indicate that it was in use at the time the common was established and this would perhaps favour the idea of an early medieval date for the common (Pearson and Pollington 2004, 19–23, 49).

The origins of town commons

The antiquity of town commons has long been appreciated: 'When an American visitor asked Freeman, the Regius Professor of Modern History at Oxford, to show him the most ancient monument in Oxford, Freeman walked him out to Port Meadow' (Hoskins and Stamp 1963, 12). However, the origins of urban commons (*see* Chapter 1) are, with few exceptions, almost wholly obscure. Indeed, the origins of commons – both urban and rural – are not entirely clear. 'Common pastures' are mentioned in the Domesday survey of 1086 but it has been argued that this was not technically 'common' because there was plenty of land available for all purposes and therefore no need for 'rights'; according to this scheme it was the creation of fields on waste through the later medieval period and the consequent reduction of 'common' land that led to the development of 'rights' from customary practices (Short and Winter 1999, 616). This idea is questionable, especially in light of recent evidence that has reinforced a view that the creation of medieval

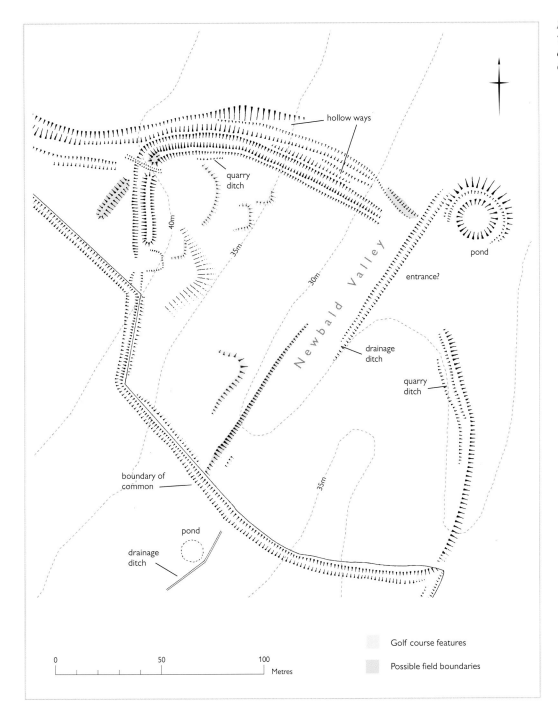

Figure 2.8
The Newbald Valley
enclosure, Westwood
Common, Beverley.

field systems, in the English Midlands at least, belongs to a period before the Norman Conquest, probably during the 8th and 9th centuries (Hall 1981; *see also* Kerridge 1992, 22–3 for the example of Brandon). Furthermore, archaeological research over the last 50 years has demonstrated that from at least the second millennium BC Britain was well populated and agriculturally fully exploited. The assumption that there was 'plenty of land' available at the time of Domesday must therefore be challenged, though of course pressure on land increased during subsequent periods of population growth. Common grazing over pasture and waste was certainly established and is documented at least a hundred years before Domesday in some places, such as the West Midlands, Dartmoor and The Weald (Hooke 1981, 58; Thirsk 1984, 36; Everitt 2000, 215) and, in an urban context, at Wilton for instance.

It has also been suggested that the frequent Old English *leah* place names of Surrey refer to areas of common grazing that must therefore, if this idea is correct, have been established in the early medieval period (Smith 2005). Warner (1987) has argued that clayland common boundaries in Suffolk are derived from Roman boundaries. It is clear that common rights did not originate in royal or feudal grants but in earlier – perhaps much earlier – agricultural practices (Thompson 1991, 133).

Can the origins of commons in a specifically urban context be pushed back further? The examples of Port Meadow, Oxford (*see* pp 5 and 16), and Wilton show that Anglo-Saxon towns were supplied with commons. Wilton's common meadow, mentioned in a charter of King Edgar (959–75), was divided between the burgesses, the nunnery and others. Because Wilton was a royal foundation attached to a royal vill its common fields were in the gift of the king (Haslam 1984, 127–8); however, it is possible that even this – the earliest documentary record of an urban common – represents an even older agricultural practice appropriated by the king. The 'port' (= market) element in the name of an urban common itself suggests an Anglo-Saxon origin (Haslam 1984, 117); examples occur at Port Field (later Carme Field), Cambridge; Portfield, Chichester; Port Down Common (now Hungerford Common), Hungerford; Portmannesheath, Malmesbury; and Portfield, Marlborough, for instance, as well as Portholme Meadow, Huntingdon, and Port Meadow, Oxford. Southampton Common too, though it was not formally registered until the 13th century (Platt 1976, 50–1), may have existed by the early medieval period. The Court Leet mound – known as 'Cut Thorn' – on the northern edge of the common is suggestive of early medieval origins. This still stands as a rectangular earthwork platform standing 0.8m above the present ground level, with slight traces of a surrounding ditch – a rare survival. There is abundant evidence that many animals were brought into Saxon Southampton 'on the hoof' and consumed in the town (Bourdillon 1988), but whether the common was the place of origin or a gathering place for those animals is not known. Incidentally, although it would seem 'common sense' that town commons should be used to graze animals being brought into market from the hinterland, this is never mentioned, as far as we are aware, in the documents.

Did Roman towns have commons? It is legitimate to push the question back to the very origins of urbanisation in this country, even if in a different legal and tenurial framework. Could Lincoln's commons, for instance, be descended from Roman 'commons'? If one of the main reasons for the existence of urban commons in the medieval and post-medieval world was to provide safe grazing for the citizens' draft animals, this need would also have been manifest in Roman towns. Open grazing space within or adjacent to the urban core would have been required (*see*, for instance, Willis 2007, 151 and 153 on agricultural activity in Roman towns) but this need not, of course, have been 'common' in any sense. It could have been provided by the urban authority or by private enterprise on a cash basis.

In many cases, as noted in Chapter 1, though charters claiming to establish common rights survive from the 13th century, they do not truly mark the beginning of these commons. They are, rather, confirming rights and practices which may have existed for hundreds, if not thousands, of years. Sudbury's commons, 'given' to the burgesses by Richard de Clare in 1262, had the same acreage as the land belonging to the burgesses and St Gregory's Church at the time of Domesday, which suggests that de Clare's grant was a confirmation of existing practice established by the 11th century (French 2000, 177, n38). At Halesowen, when the borough was established during the reign of Henry III, the burgage holders were granted 'the local privilege of common of pasture throughout Halesowen Manor...' (*VCH Worcs III* 1913, 140), which sounds like the extension of an existing and possibly ancient arrangement to a new group of inhabitants. It is, as Thompson puts it, not a right of common graciously instituted by a Norman monarch or lord (in this case Halesowen Abbey) but one which they have, rather, regulated and curtailed (1991, 133) by that word 'privilege'. The argument about what is a privilege granted by the powerful and what is a right belonging to the poor is one that has continued throughout the history of common lands (eg Birtles 1999, 84–5).

However, in some instances, exceptional circumstances (such as the reclamation of land) have led to the documented establishment of commons that are certainly new rather than based on more ancient arrangements. Lydd is a town built on a shingle bank and its commons – the East and West Ripes – are on land reclaimed from the sea during the medieval period. Similarly, The Roodee at Chester was salt marsh in the Roman period and was still covered by every tide until the 13th or 14th century (*VCH Ches V* 2005, 298).

Despite the relative paucity of historical evidence, there are some clues as to the origin of urban commons, including perhaps some of the earlier features discussed above – Petersfield lies on the greensand fringe of The Weald, a narrow strip known for its prehistoric barrow cemeteries and which gave rise to numerous common grazing lands, such as Iping Common, Duncton Common and Selham Common, rural commons that also have Bronze Age barrow cemeteries. The greensands, with their thin acidic soils, are of low agricultural potential, hence their use in historic times as heaths and commons. Limited evidence from environmental archaeology suggests that these geological zones were already developing as areas of rough grazing in the Bronze Age (Field 1998, 313–14; Graham *et al* 2004). The two facts of Petersfield having a barrow cemetery and being built over common land may therefore be connected, for Petersfield Heath Common was not an urban common in origin. Petersfield was built as a new town, probably in the 12th century, on the common of the village of Buriton. This is by no means rare. Similar situations of medieval new town construction on commons exist at Chelmsford, Hedon, Liverpool, Poole and Wymondham, for instance (Hoskins and Stamp 1963, 38–42). Other towns began life on existing commons, not as planned new developments but more humbly as squatter settlements; for example this is the case for Coalville and Whitstable (Everitt 2000, 218), and in the West Midlands conurbation (Large 1984, 170). Between the 17th and mid-19th centuries it was elegant spa towns and seaside resorts – Brighton, Tunbridge Wells, Harrogate, Bournemouth – that were as likely as industrial conglomerations to occupy existing commons (Hoskins and Stamp 1963, 41–2).

No matter how early the commons may have come into existence their primary purpose was to provide grazing and the choice to create and maintain them must have been deliberate. In discussing the 17th-century topography of Sheffield, Scurfield describes the greens and wayside commons as 'a sort of intercellular cement between blocks of fields, often conveying the impression of being the residuum of land left by chance when the latter were roughly carved out by unsighted survey from woodland' (1986, 163). His figure 4 (part of which is reproduced here as Fig 2.9) gives a good example of the 'intercellular cement' but even here, whether they were 'left by chance' or by more deliberate choice is open to question. After all, it is not really conceivable that a gap could be left between two blocks of fields by accident – it requires the construction of two walls rather than one.

Figure 2.9
Part of Sheffield in 1637 showing areas of common grazing land, greens and waysides between the town's fields.
[After Scurfield 1986, fig 4]

3

Farming on town commons

Prior to the Industrial Revolution, the separation between work and natural resources, or between English towns and the countryside, was less marked than it is today. Research has shown that the importance of urban agriculture and agrarian resources has been underestimated, as has their survival and significance into the 'modern' period. The majority of 17th- and early 18th-century towns had small populations, which were extended over limited geographical areas and immersed in the agrarian life of their rural surroundings (French 2000, 171). Most had common grazing and other agricultural land where townspeople kept livestock and took seasonal agricultural work (Glennie and Whyte 2000, 173). Even in manufacturing or commercial towns where farming was not central to the economy and few cultivated land in the fields, it was usual for freemen or all inhabitants to have rights to common pasture. Common meadows provided both grazing and hay essential for overwintering cattle. Occasionally, particularly during times of hardship, these common meadows and pastures were temporarily cultivated to increase food production. They also generated revenue, with payments for grazing contributing to town coffers and the town paying an amount to non-grazing commoners in lieu of their rights not being exercised. On some commons the rights not taken up by commoners could be leased out to non-commoners, but on others grazing was exclusively the preserve of the commoners.

During the 19th century, one of the most remarkable social changes in Britain was the congregation of the majority of the population into large cities and the creation of the totally 'urban' environment which followed (Mellor 1976, 1, 109). Within these 'modern' towns, even after the development of railways and trams, horses continued to be used for transport and open space was still needed for their grazing. Urban commons served as a municipal pound in which cows could graze securely and in which horses could be rested overnight when not employed during the day.

Cultivation

Cultivation, above any other agricultural use, has left the most tangible evidence for post-medieval farming on urban commons. From the late 17th century onwards good local markets for grain could be found among the populations of industrial towns (Large 1984, 171, 180) and, although self-sufficiency in corn production was neither desirable or necessary for commercial towns, the creation of a supply to supplement poor relief would have been an attractive idea in times of social instability (Smith 2004, 43). Urban commons were also cultivated in times of war when food supplies from overseas could not be relied upon and during other national emergencies such as crop failure. One key period was during the Revolutionary and Napoleonic wars against France (1793–1815), when a rise in the price of corn followed bad harvests in 1809 and 1811. Cultivation earthworks of this period are typified by 'narrow' ridge-and-furrow, produced by ploughing with heavy horses, leaving parallel straight ridges alternating with furrows no more than 5m apart. York's Hob Moor was one amongst a number of urban commons used for cultivation during this period and long lines of narrow ridge-and-furrow can still be seen across large areas (ibid, 41–3; Fig 3.1).

Kendal Fell was also cultivated during this period. Here earth and stone boundaries, 1 or 2m wide and up to 0.6m high, delimit an area of narrow ridge-and-furrow, with furrows 2 to 3m apart. These earthworks are the remains of a short-lived field system created before 1788 and worked until the later years of the

Napoleonic wars (Elsworth 2005b, 36). Further cultivation earthworks of the same period may be seen on Walmgate Stray, York (Pollington 2004, 12–13) and West Common, Lincoln (Brown 2003, 7). Newcastle Town Moor is archaeologically important since it affords us the opportunity to study two contrasting systems of broad and narrow ridging, both in the field and with historic maps and plans, for example Oliver's 1852 plan of Newcastle (Soc of Antiq Newcastle: PM32). Here ridge-and-furrow is visible over large areas of the surface (Lofthouse 1995, 39–41).

During the 20th century wartime blockades initiated a government-backed programme aimed at the expansion of arable land. First and Second World War cultivation has usually left little archaeological trace, although it may account for the absence of earlier remains on some urban commons. Westwood Common, Beverley, was cultivated during the First World War, but the consequent ridging that appeared on aerial photographs of 1917 is no longer evident. Large areas of urban common land were given over to allotment grounds under the First World War Defence of the Realm Act, or as part of the Second World War 'Dig for Victory' campaign – four further areas on Westwood Common were brought into cultivation to support this campaign during the Second World War. Three of these areas have sequences of long, straight parallel banks no more than 0.5m high (Pearson and Pollington 2004, 40). Low Moor Allotments were probably laid out across the north-eastern corner of Walmgate Stray, York, during the First World War (Pollington 2004, 14), while allotments were created on Newcastle Town Moor during the Second World War. Some of those on the Town Moor are no longer cultivated but earthwork features remain. On the northern part of Hunter's Moor in Newcastle, two intermittent parallel banks are the remains of raised track-ways that ran between Second World War allotment plots, while on Little Moor contemporary allotments covered a triangular area

Figure 3.1
Lines of narrow ridge-and-furrow across the ancient common of Hob Moor, York, survive from its cultivation during the late 18th- and early 19th-century wars with France. Broader medieval ridge-and-furrow can be seen in the bottom right-hand corner, beyond the former city boundary. [NMR 17707/02]

bounded by low banks and subdivided into regulation 25m × 10m (70ft × 33ft) plots by slight ditches (Lofthouse 1995, 48).

Not all ridge-and-furrow found on urban commons represents short-term cultivation and any interpretation needs to be cautious. In some instances the presence of ridge-and-furrow or field boundaries on urban commons indicates that they have expanded or their boundaries have been otherwise altered to incorporate former arable fields. On Stafford Common, for example, narrow ridge-and-furrow, earthen field banks and strip-lynchets represent common arable land granted to the householders and commoners of the town in 1801 to compensate for the loss of their grazing lands to enclosure (Fig 3.2). In Worcester the Pitchcroft comprises two historically different elements, one of which, 'The Moor', was arable land prior to its addition to the common, probably in 1775 (Hodgetts 2003, 25). Here narrow ridge-and-furrow is also evident.

Grazing

Grazing was, arguably, the most important historical use of urban commons. It leaves few, if any archaeological remains, but the early origins of some urban commons as ancient pastures can be traced through documentary

Figure 3.2
This 1954 photograph shows ridge-and-furrow of former arable fields that became part of Stafford Common following the enclosure of the town's common pastures in 1801.
[RAF/540/1460 V 19, 28 Oct 1954]

sources and other evidence (*see* pp 17–19). Pasture rights over manorial waste attached to the tenements of freeholders existed by at least the medieval period. Additional rights granted by charter and not attached to property were said to be held 'in gross'. In corporate towns these were frequently exercised by the mayor and burgesses or freemen of the borough (Maidlow 1867, 11; French 2003, 41).

In areas of England where large tracts of open waste existed, these usually provided grazing lands for nearby towns. In the northern uplands, for example, common pasture was readily available on wide expanses of moor and fell, and grazing rights were exercised over these areas by residents of nearby towns. A particular type of 'urban common' has been identified with areas of medieval transhumance in the Pennines, Cumbria, Northumberland, the Malverns, the Mendip Hills, Exmoor and the Chilterns (French 2000, 176). In West Yorkshire, Ilkley Moor and Holme Moor (also known as Common Heath), southeast of Wakefield, were used for common grazing. A similar situation occurred in coastal areas, where town grazing lands lay on expanses of salt marsh and coastal plain adjacent to towns. The East Anglian Fens and the heaths of southern England once served a similar purpose, the former having been lost to 18th-century land improvement and the latter being fragmented by more recent housing development.

Wherever the countryside was suitable for cultivation or where pasture was rich, the pressures to enclose land were high and consequently the waste ground available to towns for grazing stock became more limited. The situation of most major towns close to rivers meant that the flood plain, being unsuitable for either urban expansion or cultivation, frequently served as the town common. Such lands provided good alluvial grazing, enriched periodically by the deposition of river silts. Seasonal flooding from the Rivers Severn and Avon was a problem that prevented the expansion of Tewkesbury to the west, where its common, the Severn Ham, lies (*see* Fig 8.1). During floods in 1947, the common was recorded as being below 6ft (1.8m) of water (*VCH Glos VIII* 1968, 114), surpassed only by the floods of 1760 and 2007, which reached the abbey itself. York's Knavesmire and Loughborough's Big Meadow are also prone to inundation, the latter having been managed as a flood meadow throughout its history. Although the Knavesmire provided wet pasture for cows, this was insufficient for the needs of the citizens and, like many towns, the city built up an extensive and complex system of pasturage over extramural closes and lands of neighbouring townships (*VCH York* 1961, 498). In Sudbury half-year common pasture rights (the rights to graze half-yearly on permanent pasture) also spilled over the formal bounds of the commons onto the neighbouring closes (French 2000, 196), while in many other towns pastures were intercommoned with inhabitants of neighbouring manors.

In most towns access to grazing rights became increasingly restricted over time, as areas of common pasture dwindled due to enclosure or town expansion. Population pressure also provided an impetus to limit access by making distinctions between residents and burgesses, and vesting rights in the latter (French 2003, 41). In 17th-century Hertford rights were claimed as being attached to all cottages over 30 years old, but by the early 18th century only burgage tenements or householders of the 'ancient borough' qualified (*VCH Herts III* 1912, 497). Similarly in Godmanchester, it was enacted in 1607 that only tenements existing before 28 September 1601 should have rights of common attached to them (*VCH Hunts II* 1932, 290).

In order for common pasture to be preserved, the number of grazing beasts was limited by 'stints', which specified the types of animal and numbers permitted to graze. The restriction of *levancy and couchancy* was often applied, meaning that grazing cattle had to be living in the town and able to be supported on the winter herbage and hay of the tenement to which the right was attached (Maidlow 1867, 16). Pasture rights attached to arable landholdings were also often restricted to beasts useful for tillage, namely heavy horses and oxen to draw the plough, along with cows and sheep to manure the ground. In Coventry rights were claimed to derive from a grant of 1249 reserving to the *communiariis* 'reasonable pasture' for as many beasts 'with which they may conveniently plough and carry their arable lands...' (Thompson 1991, 122), while in Marlborough burgesses of the town had the right to depasture 'rotherbeasts' (oxen) (Parliamentary Return 1870). Common grazing rights could also extend to other beasts, such as swine, goats and geese (Maidlow 1867, 14–15), though pigs were often excluded because of their destructive tendencies. On Harrogate Stray no mules, goats, swine or geese were permitted, whereas in Beverley the Archbishop of York's grant of the pasture of Beverley to the townspeople in 1379–80 reserved to him and his tenants the right to feed pigs there. Free-roaming pigs proved troublesome and in 1572 the bishop's men were ordered to ring their animals (*VCH Yorks VI* 1989, 214–15). Clitheroe Town Moors supported large numbers of geese (French 2003, 51). On Westwood and Hurn Commons in Beverley, common rights were quantified in 'cattle gates', with one cattle gate equalling an acre of land over which a cow or horse, three ewes plus lambs or four 'hogs' (short for 'hoggerel' or 'hogget', meaning a young sheep prior to first shearing) could be pastured.

A further means of reducing over-grazing of the commons was to introduce new stints or to reduce existing stints. Towards the end of the 16th century the stint at Grimsby was reduced after the enclosure of the West Marsh (Gillett 1970, 108, 187), while in the 17th century fewer cattle were permitted on the common lands of Sudbury, Oxford, Marlborough, York, Colchester, Calne and Tewkesbury. By the later 19th century, grazing schemes were set up over some urban commons by Acts of Parliament with the aim of preserving the pastures.

The cost of maintaining urban commons was often met by charging a fee for grazing. In 1295–6 burgesses in Hertford paid 4d a head to graze horses on the pasture of Hartham, 3d a head for oxen and cows, 1½d for calves and 1d for sheep. In 1384 'foreigners', by ancient custom, were also allowed to put their cattle onto the pasture at a rate of 1d a head higher than the burgesses (*VCH Herts III* 1912, 498). In Sudbury in 1644 each horse was charged at 1s for a season's grazing and each cow 10d. Charges fluctuated widely, so that in 1710–28 the cost for a single animal was never less than 3s but in 1713 this rose to 6s 6d (French 2000, 179).

From their proximity to rivers, most urban commons needed no special provision for watering stock, but ponds may be found. Westwood Common, Beverley, situated on permeable chalk, was largely devoid of surface water but had reliable springs and wells. Here a number of beast ponds are amongst the most noticeable earthwork features on the common. They are dry today but were presumably lined with clay and fed by a combination of ground seepage off the higher slopes and by underground pipes and surface drains. In their present form they probably date to the 19th century, but as established watering holes they could have origins in the medieval period and be associated with the clearance of woodland from the common. This longevity of use is evident from the deeply incised sections of hollow way leading towards several of the ponds (Pearson and Pollington 2004, 28–9). On Figham Common, Beverley, where natural ponds form in large and shallow low-lying hollows, two artificial subcircular ponds – 14.5m and 18m in diameter – have been found, one of which is connected to a complex of small drainage ditches (Pollington and Pearson 2004, 9). The remains of two ponds survive on York's Walmgate Stray (Pollington 2004, 10), while ponds in Sutton Park, Sutton Coldfield, may have medieval origins (Wager 1998, 67).

The overseers

Grazing without right and breaking of stints were frequent occurrences on urban commons and a watchful eye was needed to enforce regulations. In Coventry, from as early as the 15th century, the tendency of powerful men to run sheep on the borough commons in numbers above their entitlement was a cause for dispute (Platt 1976, 122). More unusual occurrences also needed to be prevented, such as that reported in 1681 on the Pitchcroft, Worcester, when fleeces were stolen from the backs of grazing sheep (Hodgetts 2003, 25).

Appointed commons' officers appear with a wide variety of titles such as 'pinders', 'pinners' (also known as 'pound herds'), 'herdsmen', 'neat herds' and 'shepherds', 'haywards', 'common keepers' and 'fen reeves'. These offices had precedent in manorial custom and their duties included looking after the meadows and pastures, caring for stock, impounding stray cattle (including stock grazing without right) and removing diseased animals. Many had a vested interest in detecting transgressors, since breaking stints, stocking without right, grazing out-parish cattle or pasturing cattle fully horned were all offences for which penalties included a sum for the pinder (Neeson 1993, 142). In addition to looking after livestock and enforcing regulations, commons' officials carried out works such as fencing, opening gates and keeping the pastures clean. Sudbury's commons operated under the

control of a keeper (or beadle) by the 1720s. Rules introduced in 1644–7 prohibited the planting of willow and laid down fines for overstocking, pasturing cattle without rights and turning out ungelded horses or mangy cattle. In addition to enforcing these regulations, it was the keeper's job to ensure that the gate to the commons was locked at 10pm and not opened again until 4am during the pasture season (French 2000, 178–9). In 1867 Robert Exley was appointed Herd of Alnmouth Common for the wage of 7s a week. His duties included cutting the 'Yellow Tops and Nettles, also Thistles, and the cows to be landed in the village according to the ancient custom night and morning' (*Alnmouth Common News* 1999, 2).

The tradition of common keeping continued until recent times in some towns and cities. Mrs Marjorie Bolton (*neé* Clayton) was brought up in the Common House, which still stands on the edge of Stafford Common (Fig 3.3). Both her father and great-grandfather were Common Keepers. Her father, Tommy Clayton, was well known by the townsfolk of Stafford. His job involved looking after more than 200 milking cows and 90 horses as well as making fences, maintaining a walkway, cutting down weeds, making jumps for horse races and preparing the common for special events. Until at least 1976 there was an overseer who supervised the common during the grazing season (*VCH Staffs VI* 1979, 210). On some urban commons the pastures continue to be carefully preserved. On Newcastle Town Moor,

for example, the Stewards' Committee employs four full-time agricultural workers who are responsible for the upkeep of the land, including drainage and harrowing for pasture improvement, as well as fencing and other routine maintenance (Lofthouse 1995, 48–9).

Houses on or close to the edge of urban commons were frequently provided for the accommodation of commons officials. In Beverley cottages for cowherds lay at the main entrances to the pastures; those for Figham Common and Swine Moor were built in 1824 and 1869 respectively and that for Westwood Common was rebuilt in 1856 (*VCH Yorks VI* 1989, 215). The gatehouse to Swine Moor still survives, as does the Herdsman's Cottage on Walmgate Stray, York (Fig 3.4). Situated next to

Figure 3.5
A cattle drift.

the northern entrance to the Stray, on Heslington Road, it appears on the Ordnance Survey 1st-edition 6in map of 1853. It was occupied by a herdsman employed by the Freemen of Walmgate to look after the livestock on Walmgate Stray; it is now owned by the City Council (Pollington 2004, 10). Two workers' cottages were built on Newcastle Town Moor by the Stewards' Committee to house workers employed by the freemen for various jobs involved with the upkeep of the moor. These houses became known as the 'Blue Houses' due to the regulation colour of their paintwork. One has been demolished and low banks mark the course of the wall around the property, which is visible as a rectangular platform. The other still stands on the corner of Duke's Moor – adjacent to the junction of Grandstand Road and the Great North Road – to which it has lent its name, the 'Blue House roundabout' (Lofthouse 1995, 54). Where buildings have been demolished, place-name evidence also provides clues to their former existence. In Nottingham,

where the commons were built over in the 19th century, the names 'Pinder's House Road' and 'Pinder's Street' survive as reminders of the area's past.

Where overstocking or illegal grazing was a persistent problem, 'drifts' were held, when officials drove all stock off the common pastures and herded them together into small enclosures or 'pinfolds' (Fig 3.5). Here they were counted, interlopers detected and their owners fined. Cattle grazing legally were usually identified by a town brand, although in Sudbury, by 1725, cows depastured legally were identified by wooden bobbins known as 'tottles' or 'gruggs' threaded onto their horns (French 2000, 179). On Doncaster Town Moor drifts were a frequent event during the early 17th century. In 1606 sheep were impounded in the pinfold by the mayor and others, while in 1610 the droves of cattle were undertaken by the pinder (Anon 1902, 73, 135). In Grimsby, following the enclosure of West Marsh in about 1514, illegal grazing and overstocking appears to have been a problem on the remaining commons, which were driven twice monthly (Gillett 1970, 106). Drifts were held frequently on Peterborough's commons in the 18th century; they were expensive to mount – extra men had to be employed, horses hired and informers paid for each animal they identified – but sometimes produced useful income from fines (Neeson 1993, 134–5). Illegal stocking on Lincoln's commons incurred heavy fines following a drift in 1838, but transgressions evidently continued, for advertisements appeared in county papers giving notice that cattle sent from a distance and put on the commons would be 'seized and detained for payment of the highest fee' and further drifts were held in 1839 and 1841 (Lincolnshire Archives: L1/1/9, 216, 383). On Tewkesbury's Severn Ham illegal grazing by cattle being driven from Wales was a problem identified in 19th-century posters (Fig 3.6).

Although archaeological remains associated with grazing are few, some features can be noted. Cattle pounds or pinfolds, as secure enclosures for the temporary accommodation of stray animals, have an ancient history. They were a constituent of medieval manors and early boroughs appointed their own officials to supervise them, although surviving examples most commonly date from the 17th to 19th centuries. For convenience pounds were usually situated on the edge of commons where examples may survive today. Many are square, rectangular or irregular, according to the shape of the plot of ground available, while others are circular, especially in Yorkshire, Derbyshire and Suffolk. On Hampstead Heath, London, a circular brick-walled enclosure, with the side supports for its gate fashioned from the jawbone of a whale, was built in 1787 to replace a pound removed by a man presented at the Manor Court. This can still be seen, close to Whitestone Pond. Near Southampton Common's western entrance, a square pound enclosed with stout oak posts and two iron rails also survives (Willmott Dobbie 1979, 3, 11, 33, 36). Many more examples have been destroyed. In Grimsby the name 'Pinfold Lane' is all that remains to mark the site of the pound on East Marsh (Gillett 1970, 107).

Haymaking

The hay crop was an important product of many urban commons and the period of the year for which grazing was permitted reveals a

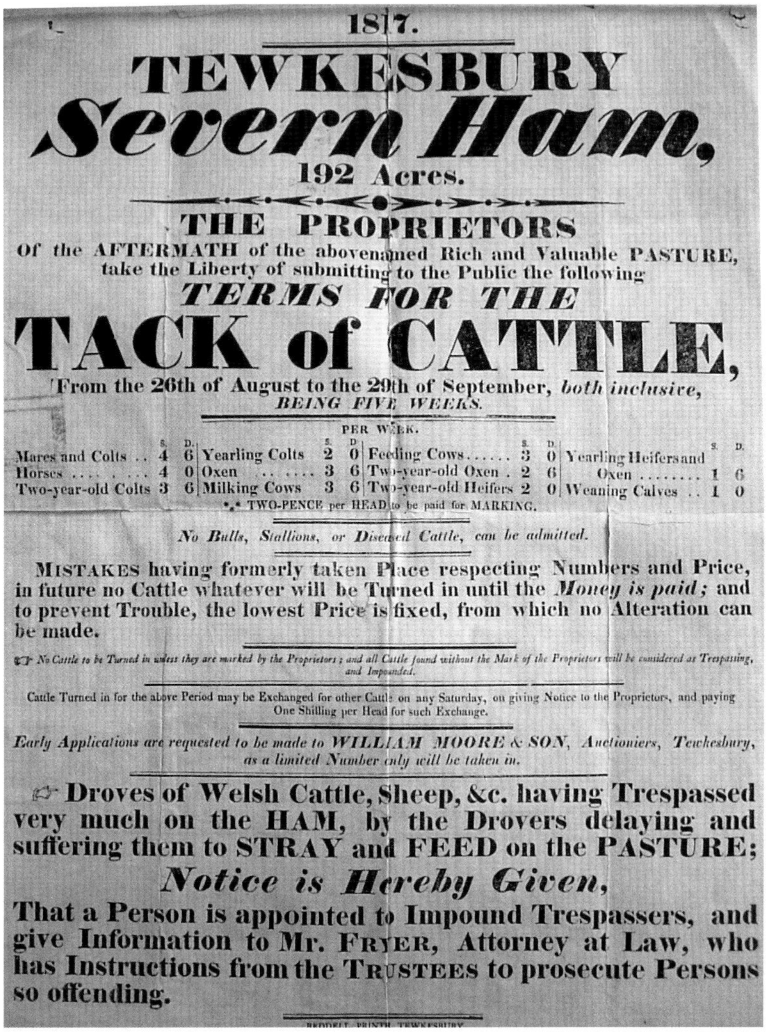

Figure 3.6
Poster advertising the terms of aftermath grazing on the Severn Ham, Tewkesbury. [Gloucestershire RO TBR/A17 1817; Reproduced courtesy of Tewkesbury Borough Council]

common's use for this purpose. Traditionally grazing was prohibited between Candlemas (2 February) and Lammas Day (12 August or 1 August after 1762). The name 'Lammas lands' was thus frequently applied to hay meadows, although the precise dates appear to have varied between individual commons. In some towns more complex arrangements occurred. In Hertford, for example, the common hay and grazing lands were subject to rotation, with King's Meads being fenced for hay every third year and a third meadow, included in King's Meads in 1331, open once every three years.

For the division of the crop, hay meadows were usually divided into strips, which were allocated each year. Strips in High Mead, the common meadow of Burford, were allocated by lots cast on 30 June each year and West Mead, Chippenham was similarly shared (Brian 1999, 45–56). Common grazing precluded the enclosure of strips by hedges or fences,

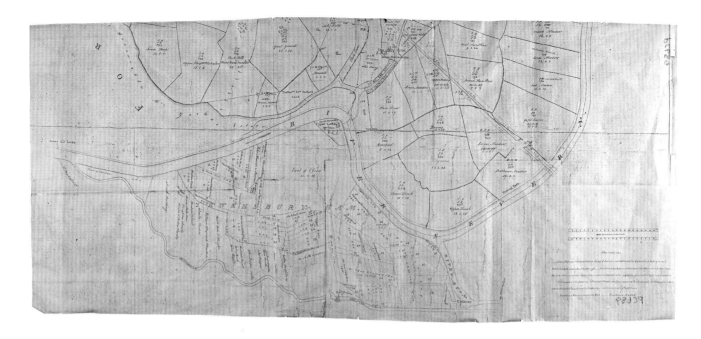

Figure 3.7
Map depicting the
ownership of strips of land
on Tewkesbury's Severn
Ham in 1792. [PC689,
Reproduced courtesy of
Gloucestershire Archives]

so their extent was marked by mere posts or stones. Linear strips were still demarcated on the Lammas lands in Godalming at the time of enclosure in 1811 (Lloyd 1992, 64–5), but they no longer survive. A late 18th-century map (Fig 3.7) shows strips on Tewkesbury's Severn Ham, with the names of their owners who sold the hay in small parcels each year; the boundaries of these strips were marked by wooden posts or stones. Mere stones on Cricklade Common are also probable hay apportionment markers, whereas wooden posts on Stafford Common are of uncertain purpose, though they may suggest that the common was used as a hay meadow.

Improving the waste

The tendency of many urban commons to waterlogging or flooding (Fig 3.8) has made them the subject of various water management systems. These are often of considerable archaeological significance, although they may have destroyed earlier deposits by cutting into them or causing their desiccation. During the 20th century, in particular, insensitive and expensive land drainage and flood defence schemes caused catastrophic damage to historic management systems (Cook and Williamson 1999, 4, 13).

Drainage systems designed to prevent the waterlogging of pasture and improve the health of grazing stock have a long history. In the medieval period communities gradually

Figure 3.8 (opposite, top)
In 1924 livestock and goods
had to be rescued when the
Three Counties Show on the
Pitchcroft, Worcester, was
flooded by the River Severn.
[From the collection of
Mr Ron Shuard]

Figure 3.9 (opposite, bottom)
Flood meadow earthworks
on King's Meads, Hertford.

combined to undertake flood defence and drainage work, which varied from major schemes to local flood alleviation carried out by manorial courts. Channels, embankments, sluices and water-lifting machines to remove unwanted water all survive as archaeological features. Figham Common, Beverley, remains partly waterlogged despite having a network of small drainage channels, which appear to have been dug as the need required, and the construction of flood banks in 1986. Some of the drains may date from as early as the 13th century, when the area was transferred to common ownership (*VCH Yorks VI* 1989, 217; Pollington and Pearson 2004, 3, 8). On Newcastle Town Moor there is archaeological earthwork evidence for late 18th- and early 19th-century land improvement. Here intakes are surrounded by shallow earthwork drains that cut across pre-existing areas of ridge-and-furrow. In intakes that enclose previously cultivated land there is no trace of later plough-ing, but where intakes only partly overlie broad ridge-and-furrow the remainder of their areas are filled with narrow ridge-and-furrow indica-tive of 18th- and 19th-century ploughing. Where the intake seems to have been on virgin ground the whole area is filled with narrow ridge-and-furrow and the block boundary in most cases corresponds with the shape (Loft-house 1995, 40–1). In the later 18th century both Figham Common and Swine Moor, Bever-ley, were placed under the jurisdiction of newly formed drainage boards. Figham Common was

FLOODED SHOW   WORCESTER JUNE 1924

cut by two drains: the Beverley and Barmston Drain, a wide channel that bears no direct part in the drainage of the common itself, and the Beverley and Skidby Drain (Pollington and Pearson 2004, 9). The New Main Drain was cut to drain Swine Moor in 1802. In York attempts had been made to drain the Knavesmire by 1649, when by-law infringements included 'blocking the common ditch leading from Knavesmire ... which overflowed the whole common, causing a loss to the whole of Micklegate ward of £50'. In the same year and in 1647, some inhabitants of Middlethorpe faced fines of £20 for not digging a ditch on the Knavesmire or cleansing a ditch leading from the Knavesmire (York City Archives: F7/205, 229).

Flood defences were also constructed on some urban commons, such as the sea wall built on the Bristol Downs by John Wallis in 1746 (Goldthorpe 2006, 37). The Severn Ham at Tewkesbury has a flood embankment alongside the River Avon; the River Lee alongside King's Meads, Hertford, is similarly embanked (Fig 3.9). In both cases the embankments are now in use as footpaths.

Reclamation and improvement of 'waste land' gathered pace in the century before 1850. During this period drainage systems were laid out across urban commons and underground drainage systems – 'bush drains' – were introduced. In the 19th century these were superseded by earthenware pipe drains (Cook and Williamson 1999, 10–12). Pipes were arranged in parallel, regularly spaced lines, connected to a main outlet, or with individual outfalls used on flat land where there might be a problem of achieving a satisfactory gradient (Castle *et al* 1984, 92–3). The first Enclosure Act for Somerset concerned the reclamation of Glastonbury's Common Moor in 1722 (Taylor 1999, 148). In Bristol an agreement was made with the commoners in 1897 to drain part of Durdham Down (Bristol RO: 34901/206). Subtle earthworks of underground drainage systems consisting of straight, shallow linear depressions leading to rivers can be seen on some urban commons, such as Southampton and Saffron Walden. Other improvement schemes were private, profit-making ventures resulting in enclosure and the loss of common rights (*see* pp 41–3).

By the 1920s further land drainage schemes were being funded by the Ministry of Agriculture and Fisheries as a means of alleviating

unemployment, while prisoners-of-war provided labour during the First and Second World Wars (Bowers 1998, 71). On Biggleswade Common, Bedfordshire, there are drainage earthworks of various dates close to the River Ivel, including 20th-century works with concrete covers and a linear embankment at least 15m wide with ditches on either side. Intensive drainage also appears in the form of closely spaced parallel ditches adjacent to a canalised section of the river (McOmish and Newsome 2006, 7).

Securing the boundaries

The boundaries of urban commons were not static and many have lost part of their area or had areas added to them in exchange for loss of common land elsewhere. In many towns rights in the common or Lammas lands were nevertheless signalled annually when the corporation and freemen rode the boundaries, trampled any corn grown in them (unless propitiated by supplies of food and ale) and tore down gates and obstructions. In Coventry the Lammas riding took place into the 19th century (Thompson 1991, 123) and records of similar ceremonies in York date back to 1374. Here two boundary stones still survive on the Knavesmire. In Bristol the ancient boundary of grazing lands, recorded in a charter of AD 883 as including part of Durdham Down, is marked by seven stones (Goldthorpe 2006, 3; Fig 3.10).

In order to prevent stock from straying onto town streets, trespassing onto private lands or

Figure 3.10
Boundary stones on
Durdham Down, Bristol.

causing damage to growing crops, urban commons needed a secure perimeter. Natural barriers, such as rivers, were sometimes adequate. Tewkesbury's Severn Ham, for example, is effectively an island, as is much of Figham Common, Beverley. Other commons were hemmed in by building development. Urban commons lacking such obstacles needed perimeter earthworks or fencing. Boundaries of commons often have a slight and not very distinctive bank and ditch, probably for supporting a perimeter hedge. Although there are no longer any common rights to graze livestock on Southampton Common, its boundary is still partly delimited by a turf bank, a ditch and boundary marker stones. These are of unknown date but may have medieval or earlier origins since there is evidence to suggest that the common was used for grazing livestock from at least the 10th century (Platt 1976, 50–1; Southampton City Council 2007, 13–14). On Westwood Common, Beverley, the boundary earthwork may also have early origins. It consists of a broad, shallow ditch about 4m wide and up to 1m deep respected by, and so likely to pre-date, medieval plough ridges outside the southern edge of the common (Pearson and Pollington 2004, 12). On some

urban commons boundary earthworks have been destroyed due to widening and metalling of roads or shrinkage of the common's area, while perimeter railings have been constructed around others. Walls and railings around Stafford Common served an additional purpose – during the early 20th century coal tar was spread on their tops by the keeper to prevent people from climbing over and entering events on the common without paying (Mrs Irene Lea, *pers comm*). To the same end, the Worcester corporation proposed new 'unclimbable' fencing for the Pitchcroft in 1895, with formal gates designed to add dignity to the approach to the common (Hodgetts 2003, 28). On Westwood Common, Beverley, formal gates and a gatekeeper's house were erected in the 19th century. The fencing of urban commons was not without problems. In Lincoln in 1836, gates straddling the turnpike roads through the town's South and West Commons were causing such delay, danger and inconvenience to stagecoaches that two lodges were erected on the West Common and one on the South Common (Fig 3.11), with the occupiers being required to open the gates for people passing through on horseback or in carriages (Lincolnshire Archives: L1/1/9, 838).

Figure 3.11
This 19th-century gatekeeper's lodge stands beside the former turnpike road that once crossed Lincoln's South Common. This road now lies on its periphery following the loss of part of the common to development.

The decline of farming on town commons

The transformation of large numbers of urban commons from farmed lands into public parks or other open urban spaces took place over a long period, but especially during the 19th century. The introduction of intensive agriculture and mechanisation caused displaced farm labourers to seek new employment in expanding industrial towns. As urban populations swelled and towns spread beyond their ancient boundaries, many town commons were lost to building development and others became truly urban, encircled by new streets and buildings. The dwindling numbers of urban commons became increasingly important as open spaces for public recreation within heavily congested towns and cities, while their value as agricultural land was limited by the strict regulations upon their use.

The requirement for provision of open spaces for public recreation in overcrowded and unsanitary towns emerged from the mid-19th century onwards. It arose from the misconception that disease was caused by air pollution, and open spaces were thus intended to provide reservoirs of wholesome air to purify the blood of the town citizens (Mellor 1976, 110). Heavy use of urban commons for leisure by town and city populations conflicted with the interests of graziers. In Worcester the grass at the Pitchcroft was seriously damaged following the County Agricultural Show and Buffalo Bill's Wild West Show in 1903. Similarly, on Grimsby's East Marsh fireworks were prohibited after squibs were let off near haystacks and every year the 'bellman' was sent round the town to cry a prohibition against anyone lighting bonfires on the Marsh on 5 November. In 1823 all ball games were also forbidden following injuries to freemen's stock (Gillett 1970, 185; see pp 63–4).

Where small arable holdings were built upon, the grounds for overwintering stock were lost and the number of people in towns requiring livestock to maintain their arable land declined (Hunter 1867, 359–60). Agriculture no longer formed an important element in the economy of growing industrial and commercial towns, and with the advent of the welfare state, motorised transport and relatively well-paid wage labour in the mid-20th century, townspeople no longer needed to keep livestock. Even where arable lands survived they could be ploughed using tractors and enriched by chemical fertilisers, so heavy horses, oxen, sheep and cattle were no longer required. By 1876 only 130 out of 2,300 ratepayers entitled to graze cattle on Stafford Common exercised their rights (VCH Staffs VI 1979, 210). In Beverley, by the later 19th century there were often 500–600 non-stockers and in 1896–7 only 143 people used their 'gates' (VCH Yorks VI 1989, 216). Grazing of Bristol's downs was also in serious decline by the later 19th century. By 1872 only 300–400 sheep were being turned out to pasture from a permitted number of at least 1,882. Grazing on Clifton Down ceased completely in the mid to late 19th century, while on Durdham Down it stopped in the 1920s and mowing has kept the area open since then. Most commons now have very few active commoners and, in some instances, none at all (Short 2000, 129).

Although custom governed the regulation and use of commons, it was not immutable and, from at least the mid-19th century, common grazing rights were frequently leased out or otherwise transferred. Money collected from graziers was distributed to non-grazing commoners. In Clitheroe those who did not possess rights were forbidden from hiring them, but in practice, 'beast gates' were traded freely among inhabitants and tenants (French 2003, 40, 51). In York freemen without stock were in the habit of selling their 'gates' to other freemen. In 1835 the Pasture Masters of Micklegate (containing Hob Moor and the Knavesmire) were accused of greatly increasing charges for pasturage in order to raise a surplus to divide among freemen without stock and freemen's widows. From 1850 onwards the principle of making payments to the non-grazing freemen of the city became accepted (VCH York 1961, 504–5).

In many towns rights were completely relinquished – usually to town corporations – in return for compensation. In Doncaster in 1893 the corporation paid compensation to commoners for their rights on Doncaster Town Moor and the herbage was thereafter leased to graziers. In 1915 rights on the Lincoln commons were also extinguished on payment of compensation to commoners and freemen, and the corporation now owns and administers the commons (Hoskins and Stamp 1963, 114). In Coventry, hemmed in on all sides by Lammas lands, the density of the town's population and the value of common lands as potential building sites increased annually. Here the freemen, after much controversy, gave up their rights in return for an allocation of land (Thompson 1991, 123).

4

From the land

A wide variety of natural resources found on urban commons have long been exploited. Stone and minerals were quarried from prehistoric times, while fuel, wood and food have been gleaned by townspeople 'since time immemorial'. For many small craftspeople urban commons yielded the raw materials used in their trades. More recently, public utility companies have found uses for town commons.

Mines and quarries

The most ubiquitous and prominent earthworks to be seen on urban commons are those created by the extraction of stone and minerals, a process that has left many urban commons with characteristic pits, mounds and quarries (Fig 4.1). The archaeology of urban commons is never more closely interlinked with the history of towns than when considering extractive industry. From their situation close to or within towns, urban commons have always been convenient places from which building materials could be readily obtained and these materials fuelled the town expansion that threatened the very survival of many urban commons.

The value of mineral resources was well recognised from early times and the rights to dig and take them were usually tightly regulated. They could be attached to an ancient tenement, held in gross or by custom of the manor and, by the 19th century, they had to be limited to be supported in law (Maidlow 1867, 20–2). It was often the case that although

Figure 4.1
Quarrying.

commoners were able to graze the land, its mineral rights were retained by the owner, usually the lord of the manor. In the case of Harrogate Stray, the Crown reserved rights to mine and forbade any digging on the common. In Beverley the question of ownership of the soil and assets other than pasturage was a contentious subject and the cause of many disputes between the corporation and the Pasture Masters until 1978, when the Chief Commons Commissioner found in favour of the corporation (*VCH Yorks VI* 1989, 216).

As a general rule, early mining and quarrying was a piecemeal and small-scale process. This type of extraction carried out by individuals, or by small numbers of people, is a feature of many areas of common pasture. On Minchinhampton Common – where quarrying is mentioned in documents from the 12th century onwards – hundreds of small pits and mounds, less than 1m wide, are scattered across part of the common. They have various configurations, but most consist of a single oval pit flanked by one or more spoil heaps. Some cut, and hence post-date, the banks of a prehistoric field system, while later pillow mounds are undisturbed. These earthworks may be linked to documentary references to inhabitants of the manor paying rent for the privilege of quarrying stone (Smith 2002, 34–5). On Kendal Fell in Cumbria, widespread earthworks of shallow quarrying also remain. Quarrying was taking place here long before 1767, when the common right of 'stone-getting' was still important enough to be preserved following enclosure (Elsworth 2005b, 11–12). On Westwood Common, Beverley, small quarries are also potentially of medieval date, since the area was quarried for limestone in the late 14th century (Pearson and Pollington 2004, 21).

Deeper and larger depressions indicate more highly organised and large-scale extraction suggesting, although not necessarily proving, a later date. The fact that small-scale extraction continued into later periods alongside industrial-scale workings, while some early quarries increased in size as they were worked and reworked over hundreds of years, means that the dating of pits and quarries is far from straightforward. In Stafford the inhabitants of the town took marl from the common on payment of 4d a load during the 1820s (Staffordshire RO: D1323/H/3, 13), while the removal of tree roots in the 18th and early 19th centuries and digging for chalk and clay has left

Beverley's Westwood Common pitted with hollows (Pearson and Pollington 2004, 26).

The type of material sought and the geological composition of an area further influences the nature of the remains, with excavations for clay and other surface materials tending to be shallow and widespread, and deep excavations being made to reach good stone, coal or minerals. Linear quarries, or rows of small pits following mineral seams, are also commonly seen.

Clay

Clay for brick-making was an important product of many urban commons, particularly during periods of town expansion. On Lincoln's West Common clay pits existed by the 16th century and earthworks of small-scale quarrying comprising small scoops, mounds and scarps can still be seen (Brown 2003, 4, 11–12). On the Pitchcroft, Worcester, small, irregular pits are the result of digging clay for the town's buildings. In 1770 a brickworks was established on the common for the building of a new infirmary. Dips and mounds at either end of Southampton Common also result from clay digging and the Hawthorns (now a wildlife centre) was built in 1712 as a brick-maker's house with a kiln, although it was later rebuilt as a town villa (Southampton City Council 2007, 14–15). Ponds may also indicate clay extraction. On Hob Moor, York, small rectangular ponds have resulted where clay was dug by hand from at least the 14th century. By the 19th century a large clay pit and brickworks with two wind pumps and a kiln had superseded these small pits (OS 6in maps 1852 and 1892). All had gone out of use by 1937, but the large pit remained until recently as Kelsey's Pond (Smith 2004, 52–4).

Sand and gravel

Sand and gravel pits have been worked on urban commons from at least the medieval period. Sand was used for cleaning and as a good abrasive for scouring pots and pans; it was also strewn onto floors to absorb dirt, dust and grease (Neeson 1993, 168). Sand and gravel were extracted from Woking's Horsell Common for many centuries and the old workings were the setting for the Martian landing in H G Wells's 1898 novel *War of the Worlds*. Many of the older houses around the common were built using local materials and sand was sold by the load until the 1960s (Horsell Common

Preservation Society). Oxford's Port Meadow and Wolvercote Common were dug for gravel during the 16th and 17th centuries, and this is still evident from the large number of irregular hollows and spoil heaps around the edges of both commons (Lambrick and McDonald 1985, 100). The remains of a small gravel quarry – measuring 30m × 20m – also survive on the north-eastern corner of Walmgate Stray in York (Pollington 2004, 21). In coastal towns commons were a source of pebbles and shingle. On part of the East Ripe, one of Lydd's two commons, there are a number of earthworks resulting from shingle quarrying.

Metal and stone

Where it was to be found, metal ores were also mined. On Clifton and Durdham Downs, Bristol, sunken areas remain from lead working. This took place from at least the 17th century, when the lords of the manor of Henbury readily leased land for lead mining, in addition to limestone quarrying and clay working (Goldthorpe 2006, 3–4).

A good supply of building stone was important for developing towns. Shrewsbury's common, which lies between the town wall and the River Severn, is aptly named 'The Quarry', after a large stone quarry in its centre (Fig 4.2). This has now been transformed into a sunken garden. Moor Park, Preston, also has extensive stone quarries that are known to have been worked before 1736, since a stray boulder from the quarrying became the starting point for horse races that began at that date.

Lime

Lime has many uses: as a constituent of cement and plaster; a wash to lighten and waterproof buildings; an agricultural dressing; for water purification and effluent treatment; for bleaching paper; and in the preparation of hides. In 1379–80, when the Archbishop of York granted Westwood Common to the town of Beverley, he retained a limekiln there. A chalk quarry on the common with one or two kilns was let by the town from at least the late 14th century. Irregular depressions c 1–2m deep, close to Westwood Common's eastern edge, were probably dug by townsfolk to obtain clay and chalk for building or other purposes and could date from the medieval period. A series of broadly crescent-shaped scoops in the hillside are also probable chalk pits (Pearson and Pollington 2004, 28).

Increased demand

During the 18th and 19th centuries the demand for stone, aggregate and limestone accelerated rapidly and earlier quarries often expanded considerably during this period. Hardcore was

Figure 4.2
An early 18th-century engraving showing Shrewsbury from the west, with a quarry situated on common land outside the town walls. The area is now a public park known as 'The Quarry'.
[Reproduced courtesy of Shrewsbury Museums]

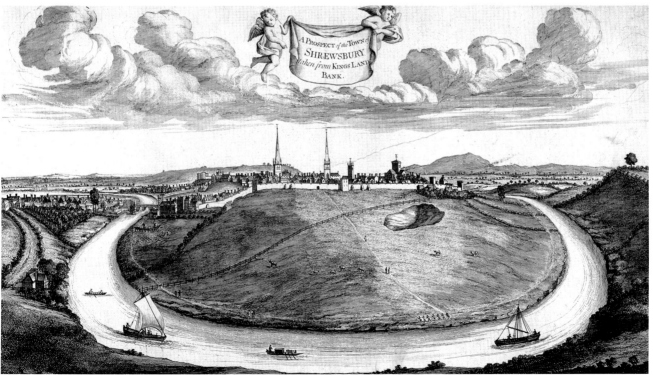

Figure 4.3
Archway leading to the
drawholes of the single
remaining limekiln on
Kendal Fell, now a
Scheduled Ancient
Monument (no. 34994).

needed for turnpike roads and railway lines, while stone was required not only for buildings but for walling erected under the enclosure acts. Limestone was also quarried in great quantities for burning to provide lime for soil improvement. On Westwood Common, Beverley, early pits were eclipsed in scale by the Limekiln Pits and two unnamed quarries towards the south-eastern corner of the common, which cover over 12ha. The approximate locations of the kilns, the last of which operated until 1812, are indicated by broad hollows (Pearson and Pollington 2004, 28). On Minchinhampton Common multi-period quarry earthworks lie across large areas. A limestone quarry cut in two by an 18th-century road and hollowed trackways, which were its precursors, may be the 'Rode Quarry' mentioned in 1516 (Russett 1991, 612). Larger pits lie beside roads at the common's edge for easy transportation of stone and on sloping ground where the best stone in the lower beds of the oolite was more easily accessed. Numerous hollowed trackways associated with the quarries cut across Minchinhampton Common (Smith 2002, 33). By the 19th and 20th centuries the scale of quarrying had increased to such an extent that it was damaging to the

pasture and to the landscape as a whole. This directly resulted in the acquisition of the common by the National Trust in order to protect it (ibid). Lime was also quarried on Kendal Fell from at least the early 18th century. Following the completion of the Lancaster Canal link to the town in 1819, the limestone quarries on Kendal Fell grew in scale, with access to cheap coal fuelling more limekilns which found a ready market for their product in the rapidly expanding town. The extraction and processing of limestone on Kendal Fell was thus inextricably linked with the creation of the modern town and the single surviving limekiln (Fig 4.3) is now a Scheduled Ancient Monument (no. 34994) (Elsworth 2005b, 11, 13, 29–32).

Coal

From at least the Middle Ages coal was taken from urban commons. Initially small quantities supplied domestic needs, but the scale of mines expanded to supply growing industries. Up until the 18th century seams of coal relatively close to the ground surface were mined using single 'bell-pits' and drift mines were dug into hillsides where coal seams outcropped. Early pits, lacking drainage or roof supports, were shallow, but by the early post-medieval period larger and deeper mines with timber roof supports were being worked. As mining techniques improved still further, from the mid-15th to the 19th centuries, pillars of coal were left to support roofs. Diagnostic features of this 'pillar-and-stall' mining are shaft heads arranged in a widely spaced grid pattern and ground subsidence following the removal of roof supports. The introduction of drainage pumps made it possible to reach yet deeper seams. In Newcastle upon Tyne the production of coal has been closely linked with the town's development for seven centuries. Here the mines were run by a common council in order to supply the citizens of the town with coal. On Newcastle Town Moor distinctive ring-banks of spoil remain from early bell-pit mines, which can be seen in lines following coal seams. These date from the medieval period. On Nuns Moor, four shaft heads form a square and on the central part of the moor seven shaft heads lie in a grid formation indicative of the pillar-and-stall technique. Collieries from the 19th century and later, along with early 20th-century opencast mining remains, are also evident, representing an almost complete coal-mining history in the field archaeology of Newcastle Town Moor (Fig 4.4). A relative dating sequence may be deduced from the earthwork remains since the shaft heads of later periods tend to have larger spoil heaps than those around early bell-pits, resulting from their greater depth. The layout of the shaft heads and their relationship to other features also give clues to their date (Lofthouse 1995, 21–2).

Transport

Many urban commons were traversed by roads. Both Roman roads and unmetalled trackways, possibly of prehistoric and medieval date, are all evident in the archaeological remains found (*see* pp 14–15). Multiple sunken trackways often run parallel to each other where they bypassed areas of muddy ground. Good examples can be seen at Corfe Common where Purbeck marble, extracted from quarries just to the south of the common, was taken across the common into the town for processing. This has resulted in the development of a series of well-defined, braided, V-shaped hollow ways (*see* Fig 1.1). These are too narrow for wheeled transport but were possibly formed by dragging the stone on sledges. These route ways can

plausibly be dated to the medieval period when the marble industry in Corfe reached its zenith (Fletcher 2003, 10–11, 13–14). With the introduction of turnpike roads in the 18th century, some of these early route ways were metalled and remain in use today, with the earthworks of their former diverging courses running alongside them. From this period onwards urban commons became a convenient open corridor for the routes of new canals, roads and railways into towns. In turn these provided transport, which allowed extractive industries on urban commons to expand their output beyond what was needed for local use. Material for road, rail and canal building projects was often extracted from the commons themselves. Hungerford Common, for example, has quarries that probably relate to the construction of the canal and railway nearby (Newsome 2005, 21). Commons were often bisected by these developments. In 1818 Camberwell New Road was built across Kennington Common, London. Similarly, in 1850, the East Coast main line railway was constructed across Biggleswade Common, cutting it in two. After protests by graziers an arch was constructed for the movement of grazing cattle.

Figure 4.4
Earthwork remains of early coal mines on Newcastle Town Moor. Shaft heads 1–5 are bell-pits exploiting a seam; 6–11 probably represent later pillar-and-stall mining. A and B are the prehistoric or Romano-British enclosures described in Chapter 2 (see Fig 2.5). The small rectangular earthworks overlying the earlier line of the racecourse are golf tees.

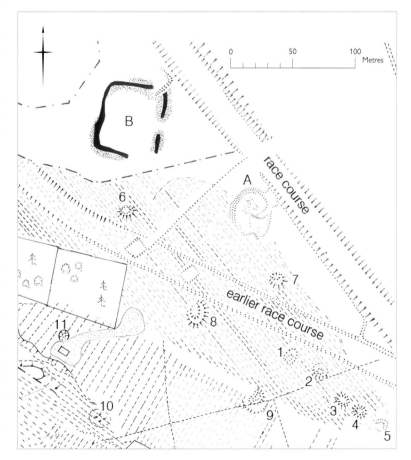

Estovers

Where urban commons included woodland or heath, common of estover – rights to take wood and other materials – were frequently exercised. The four main categories were 'fire-bote', 'plough-bote', 'house-bote' and 'hedge-bote' (wood for fire, agricultural implements, house repairs and fences respectively). While turbary and common in the soil are frequently documented as damaging to common pasture, so estovers needed to be limited in order to prevent damage to woodland. Beverley's Westwood Common was once wooded with oak and ash trees. The underwood was cut regularly for faggots and bracken was gathered by the burgesses. In the Middle Ages trees from Westwood Common were sold, used to repair town property or were felled and stolen by townspeople. From the 16th century onwards large-scale felling of the woods occurred, despite the establishment of 'haggs' (coppices) in which regrowth was protected and cut in turn. By 1765 very few trees were left on the common. On Figham Common and Swine Moor, Beverley, willow loppings for faggots were sold by the burgesses and rushes were also cut (*VCH Yorks VI* 1989, 217).

Before the introduction of coal power and the supply of gas and electricity to towns, combustible material was required by industry and households. Fallen wood, turf, gorse, peat, bracken and leaves were all dried and used as fuel. Almost anything could be burned, including tree roots and woodcutting debris (Neeson 1993, 160). On Greenham Common, Newbury, rights of estover included taking materials for fuel and fencing, and bracken for bedding. The burgesses of Poole in Dorset also had rights on Canford Heath to take heather and furze for fuel (Hoskins and Stamp, 1963, 39). Thinner branches were commonly used for bean sticks and brushes. On St John's Lye in Woking, rights of estover included bracken, pea and bean sticks, kindling wood, dead birch trees and roof timbers with a trunk diameter of up to 9in (230mm) (Aitchison *et al* 2000, Surrey CL116). On Ditton Common, Esher, a right of estover again specifies wood up to 6in (150mm) in diameter (Thompson 1991, 145).

Raw materials taken from urban commons for other purposes included bracken, furze, reeds and weeds, which were used for animal fodder and bedding. Bracken was also suitable for packaging or haystack bases and its ash was used in glass-making and bleaching. On wet commons where reeds, rushes and grasses were abundant, reed was valued as thatch for roofs, hayricks and clamps of crops and vegetables. Rushes could be woven into baskets, mats, hats, chair seats and toys, and, like reed, could be used for agricultural thatch. They were also used as bedding, netting in wall plaster, wrapping for soft cheese and rush lights. Nothing was wasted – even loose sheep's wool caught on thorn bushes was woven into blankets and clothes (Neeson 1993, 167–8).

Raw materials from urban commons provided livelihoods for some town craftspeople. A woodturner and wooden shovel maker worked on Berkhamsted Common and the principal industries of the town included lacemaking and straw-plaiting, leather-working, wood and metal crafts, and brick-making, all of which used produce from the Chilterns commons (Everitt 2000, 233). In Stamford a basketmaker named George Ratcliffe had a holding on the common which was an osier bed (Elliot 1972, 165). The livelihoods of these craftspeople depended upon commons while other townspeople supplemented often meagre incomes by selling the materials they gathered (Neeson 1993, 169).

Turbary

Turf and peat were taken for roofing, making walls and for fuel, although they never became an important fuel for industry, other than tin-making (Rackham 1986, 318). The right of turbary (the right to cut turves or peat) could only be attached to land with a house upon it, as turves were wanted to burn in the hearth; however, if the house was demolished, the right still applied to the land it had occupied (Maidlow 1867, 18–19). Common of turbary was usually subject to fixed limits in order to prevent the destruction of pasture. On Banstead Heath, Reigate, there were rights to dig peat and turf, and to collect herbage and wood providing 'it is removed on one wheel' (Aitchison *et al* 2000, Surrey CL109), while on Ormskirk Moss it was decreed in 1539 that no tenant should dig for turves for more than two days (*VCH Lancs III* 1907, 264). During the 19th century, when attempts were made to define ancient rights and customs more clearly in law, the rights of manorial tenants to take an unlimited amount of turf from Hampstead Heath for their own use was condemned, while a right attached to an ancient house on the heath to carry away as many turves as two men could dig in a day each year was allowed, as a finite amount, although it did not appear that the turves were being used in the house itself (Maidlow 1867, 19). By the middle of the 19th century the cheapness of coal meant that turves were hardly worth digging for fuel, except in places like Godalming where its inland position made coal expensive due to the numerous carriage tolls payable during its transport (ibid, 18, 183).

Earthwork remains of turf and peat extraction on urban commons are yet to be discovered, although they are common elsewhere, particularly on upland areas. The term 'cutaway' is used to describe land left over after peat or turf has been removed. Cutting by hand is represented by rectangular depressions and water-filled hollows on peat moors. These are usually poorly drained and have a residual depth of up to 1.5m. They may be accompanied by peat-drying platforms or huts. Large-scale production is less easy to identify since it results in sequential lowering of the total area.

Food and flowers

The variety of wild plants and fruits which could be gathered on urban commons provided a welcome supplement to the diets of many town dwellers (*see* Fig 1.4). Foods collected included herbs for cooking and medicine, nuts, mushrooms and leaf vegetables. Fruits such as berries, apples, haws and rosehips were also collected. Although home consumption was the norm, a ready market could be found for produce from urban commons. Bulrushes from Kelsey's Pond on Hob Moor, York, for example, were taken each Christmas to a chemist who paid 2s 6d a dozen for the seed heads, which were used as 'snow effect' decoration in the shop window (Smith 2004, 93).

Rights to take meat were often recorded and the right to fish (piscary) was applied to many riverside commons, but for most their taking was a de facto right enjoyed by ancient custom. The taking of wildfowl and rabbits was common practice and skins, bird quills and feathers were all used. On Figham Common and Swine Moor in Beverley, fishing and fowling were enjoyed by the burgesses or were let, while on Westwood Common woodland provided cover for game birds, allowing several 'cock shoots' to be leased by the corporation (*VCH Yorks VI*

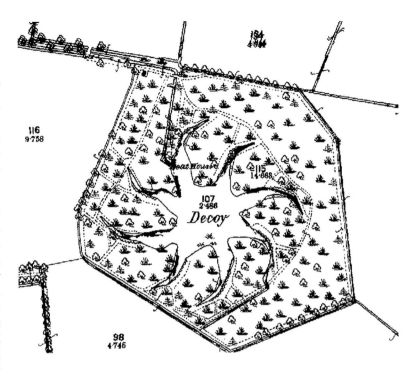

1989, 217). Where sophisticated methods were used to entrap wildfowl, archaeological traces sometimes survive. In the 18th century decoy ponds replaced decoy cages or tunnels of net as a means of enticing and entrapping ducks. Most of Peterborough's Borough Fen has been enclosed and drained, but a 17th-century duck decoy pond survives (Darby 1965, 92, 154–60; Fig 4.5). This decoy, which consists of eight pipes radiating out from a central pond, is the oldest duck decoy still in use in Britain. It is now used as a ringing station; wildfowl landing on the pond are enticed through the pipes and caught in nets at the far end.

Fine examples of 'pillow mounds' in which rabbits were farmed can also be seen on urban commons. Pillow mounds often appear in groups. They are generally uniform in height and width, and their surrounding ditches are narrow and usually extend around the ends of the mounds. Some pillow mounds have cross-shaped linear grooves on their surface from collapsed artificial burrows. Occasionally circular examples are found, which may be confused with round barrows. On Minchinhampton Common there are over 60 pillow mounds, each approximately 5m wide and varying considerably in length between 60m and 12m (Smith 2002, 27; *see* Fig 2.4). On Figham Common and Swine Moor, Beverley, further examples may be seen. Most examples

Figure 4.5
A 17th-century duck decoy pond, shown on the Ordnance Survey 1st-edition map of 1887, survives on land that was once part of Peterborough's Borough Fen. The fen is now entirely enclosed.
[© Crown Copyright and database right 2009. All rights reserved. Ordnance Survey Licence number 100019088.]

date from between the 17th and 19th centuries, after which rabbits had become hardy enough to flourish in the English countryside without protection and they were no longer a luxury but a staple food for the poor (Rackham 1986, 48).

Miscellaneous industrial and domestic activities

Clothes drying, both commercial and domestic, was a further use to which urban commons were put (Fig 4.6; *see also* Fig 5.3). Around wool-producing towns commons were the sites of tenter grounds for drying and stretching woollen cloth. In Kendal woollen cloth-making was the town's principal industry from at least the medieval period and, by 1614, tenter frames were positioned along the edge of Kendal Fell (Phillips 1984, 112; Elsworth 2005b, 6, 12). Kendal Fell continued to be used for this purpose following enclosure in 1767, but the frames were gradually removed as the industry declined due to mechanisation in the late 19th century. In the 16th century the corporation of

Bristol acknowledged a duty to protect Brandon Hill and to permit free exercise, clothes drying and 'other business'. Some urban commons continue to provide open spaces for town residents to dry washing, a practice with long traditions. Common rights to hang out washing on Bradford's Baildon Bank and Moor were registered in the 1980s, while on Cotmandene Chart in Dorking there are washing lines for residents of adjacent flats (Aitchison *et al* 2000, Surrey CL36).

In Beverley the corporation ran several windmills on Westwood Common from the 16th century. Black Mill, built before 1654–5 and rebuilt in 1803, still stands (Fig 4.7; *see also* Fig 5.5) and the lower part of the 'Anti-mill', built in 1800 as a cooperative venture, survives as part of the golf club house (*VCH Yorks VI* 1989, 218).

Urban commons have also provided stopping places for itinerant people, including Gypsies, unemployed labourers seeking work in the town and tramps. This could lead to problems, as at Dewsbury (*see* p 8) or at

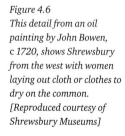

Figure 4.6
This detail from an oil painting by John Bowen, c 1720, shows Shrewsbury from the west with women laying out cloth or clothes to dry on the common.
[Reproduced courtesy of Shrewsbury Museums]

Warminster where squatters on the common were notorious in the 18th and early 19th centuries, though the hamlet (now called New Town) had been made respectable by the 1830s (*VCH Wilts VIII* 1965, 96).

Public utilities

As town populations grew, urban commons became the sites of pioneering schemes designed to bring clean water supplies into urban areas. One such scheme took spring water from King's Meads, Hertford, to London via an aqueduct named the 'New River' (Figs 4.8, 4.9 and 4.10). This remarkable aqueduct

was begun in 1609 and originally extended for 39 miles along the Lee Valley. It was carefully engineered, with the total fall on its entire length being only 5.8m. The supply was supplemented later by water from the River Lee and Marble Gauge was erected in 1770 to control this. In the mid-19th century the amount of water taken was doubled by the construction of pumping stations to take water from deep wells alongside the river and further boreholes were sunk in the 1990s to ensure that the system remained an essential part of London's water supply. The townspeople of Hertford had no access to the supply and in 1708 the corporation instead leased land on Hartham Common to a contractor who pumped water into the town. Only wealthy households could afford the supply, which was shockingly contaminated and became implicated in outbreaks of typhoid, cholera and malaria. The corporation later bought and took over the supply, which remained the only source of piped water to the town until Port Vale Reservoir was built in 1862 (Page 1993, 137–8).

During the 19th century municipalities began to show increasing concern over facilities for the health and recreation of citizens. The reasons for this are complex, but elements of compulsion were provided by the public health movement (Mellor 1976, 110). By the late 18th and early 19th centuries conditions within most towns were overcrowded and unsanitary. The practice of throwing refuse from windows onto streets created what has been described as 'an intolerable rookery of humanity established on a dunghill' (Watson 1960, 523). There were few

Figure 4.7
Black Mill, Westwood Common, Beverley, during an English Heritage survey of the common.
[© Tony Bartholomew]

Figure 4.8
Chadwell Spring, the original source of Hertford's 'New River', yields up to 4.3 mega-litres of water per day, rising in a 30m-wide circular basin known as 'The Banjo'. This local stone monument is inscribed with historic dates and river distances.

Figure 4.9
Hertford's 'New River' was built 1609–13 to take fresh water from Hertfordshire springs to London. Thames Water still uses it as a source of drinking water for London and a footpath has been created along its course. The New Gauge Building, in the distance, was constructed in 1856 to regulate the amount of water taken to feed the 'New River' from the River Lee behind it.

drains or sewers and outbreaks of disease were frequent and widespread. In 1842 the government appointed a Royal Commission to look into 'the State of Large Towns and Populous Districts'. This examined the water supplies of 50 large towns and reported that in 31 cases they were insufficient or impure. An act of 1866 eventually compelled local authorities to provide sanitary inspectors and allowed central government to insist upon the provision of sewers and a good water supply (Woodward 1962, 463–5). Land for such works could be taken without the agreement of owners or commoners. In 1868, for example, the East London Waterworks Company issued a notice to the commoners of Tottenham regarding compensation for rights over land they were compulsorily acquiring (London Metropolitan Archives: ACC/1016/485).

It was against this background that urban commons became the catchments and storage sites for town water supplies, causing reservoirs

or their remains to be typical features of urban open spaces. On Minchinhampton Common an irregular polygonal platform standing 0.4–0.6m high, with the remains of a stone wall visible around its edge, is the disused reservoir built by the Stroud Water Company before 1922 (Russett 1991, 66). A further reservoir is still in use and surrounded by metal paling (Smith 2002, 39). Water was, and still is, also collected on large upland commons adjacent to urban conurbations – for example Wardle Common, Greater Manchester, and Whitworth and Trough Common, Lancashire, where the water authority (West Pennine Water Board) has registered rights to collect water (Aitchison *et al* 2000, CL165–6).

On some urban commons deep wells were sunk. In Southampton the city's population had outgrown its water supply by the 19th century and so an artesian well was constructed on the common to meet the increased demand. Although it was dug to 1,317ft (420m) in depth, the required flow of water never appeared. It was abandoned but the cover of the shaft can still be seen. An equally abortive attempt to locate a town water supply occurred in Stafford in 1877. Here there was a useful spin-off when bore holes on the common produced brine. This led to the opening of brine baths in the town centre, fed from a spring on Stafford Common (*VCH Staffs II* 1967, 250). The construction of water catchment works on urban commons has continued to the present day. In Bristol a concrete water tower constructed on Durdham Down in 1954 remains in use.

In addition to providing clean water supplies, urban commons have housed infrastructure for other utilities and served as a convenient depository for town waste. Sewage treatment works and rubbish tips were frequently sited on urban commons. Lincoln's West Common and the Pitchcroft, Worcester, for example, have both been used as municipal tips, while sewage purification works were established on King's Meads, Hertford; King's Marsh, Sudbury; Biggleswade Common; and Earlswood Common, Reigate. As water, gas and electricity supplies were introduced to towns during the late 19th and early 20th centuries, numerous way-leave agreements were entered into for the erection of telegraph poles, electricity cables, sub-stations and the digging of water mains across urban commons. The Tewkesbury to Cheltenham water main, for example, was laid out across the Severn Ham in 1897, 1900, 1910 and 1922 (Glos County RO: A17/3). The benefits of many of these are still enjoyed by townspeople today.

Figure 4.10
The timber-clad White House and the sluice named after it, built in 1746, on King's Meads, Hertford.

5

Defence of the realm

The military use of commons, both urban and rural, has a long pedigree. In the medieval period open spaces in towns and villages were used by archers to practise their skills and as places of assembly; however, it was not until the late 18th and early 19th centuries that there was a dramatic increase in their use for training larger formations of troops – a practice which was later formalised in many enclosure acts. Besides military training, commons have also been used for trialling new equipment and munitions; for reviews, parades and sporting events; and for sites of encampments, airfields or prisoner-of-war camps during the First and Second World Wars. In some cases large tracts of common land have been acquired on a permanent basis and camps and barracks were built there, stimulating a growth in the local community – in effect creating an urban environment. This permanent acquisition of land has also had the effect of excluding the local population from part or all of a former common, but at the same time it has often preserved them from further development and encroachment and safeguarded them as 'open space'.

Unfortunately the archaeological evidence of the military's temporary use of the commons is fragmentary by its very nature and confined chiefly to rifle ranges, trench systems, pillboxes and some encampments.

Military reviews

Although commons have been used for military reviews since at least the late 17th century, it was not until the 19th century that they became

Figure 5.1
This engraving shows a review of the Kent Volunteers, with the Royal Artillery and Marines, on Woolwich Common in 1866.
[Illustrated London News, 14 July 1866, 44]

more popular. During the early years of the 19th century the City of Lincoln Volunteer Infantry frequently paraded on Lincoln's South Common (Swallow 1999, 8; 2000, 10, 22). Later examples include Stafford, where a review was held on the common in 1864 (*VCH Staffs VI* 1979, 210).

As well as these county reviews, royal reviews were held on commons in and around London. Woolwich Common (Fig 5.1) appears to have been a favoured venue; in 1830 William IV inspected soldiers of the Royal Artillery and Royal Engineers, and five years later he reviewed nearly 3,000 troops here. A year after the coronation of Queen Victoria in 1838, a celebration was held at Woolwich, which included a procession around the town's barracks onto the common. In the same year a review was attended by about 10,000 people when a number of guests and royalty from abroad witnessed the Royal Artillery carrying out training manoeuvres, including live firing. Perhaps the grandest event – attended by Queen Victoria and Prince Albert – occurred in July 1841 (Vincent 1888, 420–4).

More poignantly, commons have been used as places where the military dead are remembered and commemorated. Tewkebury's Severn Ham, for example, has been used as an assembly point for Royal British Legion rallies, and at Berkhamsted and Maltby there are memorials to the war dead (Fig 5.2).

Military training on the commons

The earliest use of urban commons for military purposes was probably during the later Middle Ages when they were used for archery practice. English archers were renowned for their prowess with the longbow, which, in part, was attributable to the legislation that gave them the right to use lands (including, presumably, greens and commons) adjacent to every village and town for practice. In 1511 statutes were passed encouraging archery as a military exercise, which was seen as essential for the defence of the country. Under Henry VIII's law,

butts should be made in every city, town, and place according to the laws of ancient time, and that the inhabitants in every of them should be compelled to make and continue such butts, and to exercise themselves with long bows in shooting at the same, and elsewhere, on holidays and other times consistent.

(TNA: WO 32/5946; Hutchins 1863, 128)

The archaeological evidence for archery butts is rather fragmentary, with no more than 25 listed in the NMR. Whether any of these were actually on a common, or merely on another 'open space', is unclear. It is noteworthy that during our fieldwork no archery butt was positively identified on any of the urban commons although later earthworks, such as those on Lincoln's South Common, may mask them. Those that have been identified are mostly in rural settings; some have been tentatively identified from field names while others survive as earthworks (in some cases their identification confirmed by place-name evidence). Where butts survive they comprise a low circular, or elongated, mound ranging from a single example to up to four, set up to 100m apart.

Figure 5.2
War memorial on Berkhamsted Common. The inscription reads: 'In memory of the Inns of Court Officers Training Corps, who in this neighbourhood trained over twelve thousand men to serve as commissioned officers in the Great War 1914–1918, and in affectionate remembrance of the two thousand who gave their lives for their country, this monument is erected by members and friends of the Corps'.
[NMR WAR4138]

Presumably the target would be placed in front of the mound, which would act as a 'back stop' in much the same way as the considerably larger rifle butts. An example is on Beaminster Down in Dorset where, until the beginning of the 19th century, there were two butts known as Beaminster Butts (NMR: ST 40 SE 14). In some cases prehistoric round barrows have allegedly been reused as archery butts; the evidence is from place names, and although tentative, it is nevertheless plausible. At Bridlington, for example, two bowl barrows are said to have been reused in this way because they are situated on Butt Hill (NMR: TA 16 NE 16).

An early example of archery practice in an urban context is at Moorfields, which, in the 15th century, lay just beyond the walls of London (Fig 5.3). Part of the moor 'aboute and beyonde the lordship of Finsbery' was used as a practice ground in 1498 (Lambert 1921, 80). Another example is Wimbledon where, in 1625,

'the inhabitants were fined 20 shillings, for neglecting to set up or renew the "metes" or butts' on the common (Plastow 1986, 27).

Although legislation had been passed for the use of open spaces for archery since at least the beginning of the 16th century, there was no requirement to provide areas for military training for larger formations of troops. Despite this, some training undoubtedly took place on urban commons, although the requirement for specific training areas does not appear to have been of much concern until the late 18th century when there was a growing threat of French invasion. Before this time, the regular army seldom exceeded 18,000 men, who were scattered in billets in towns throughout the country, while the militia for the year 1788 totalled 30,720. The militia, which was a local force, was never assembled together except at times of national emergency, but since they were raised and officered by the local landed

Figure 5.3
This detail from the Copperplate Map *of c 1559 shows Moorfields, London, in the 16th century. Archers can be seen in several places, as can women laying out clothes, people strolling and grazing animals.*
[© Museum of London]

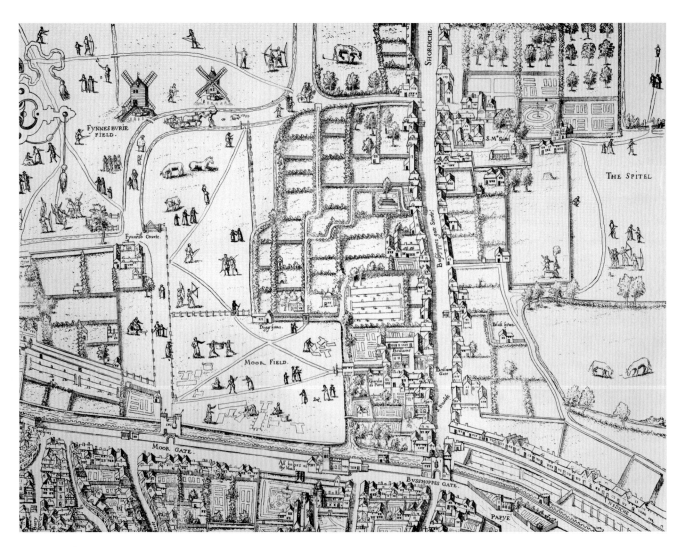

gentry, it was unnecessary to have special powers to acquire land on which to train. During any national emergency, the private rights of owners were overlooked and the military encamped on the commons without claim from the lord or commoners. After the statutory powers had ceased, the militia appears to have continued training on the common lands without compensation to the owners.

With the enclosing of the commons in the mid-19th century, it was important that there should be some provision for military training and their right was subsequently enshrined in many Enclosure Awards. At Stamford the common would be 'available for the purposes of exercise and recreation by the inhabitants of Stamford, and also for the purpose of drill or parade by any regiment or corps of the Regular Army, or of the Militia…' (TNA: WO 32/5946). Some restrictions, however, were placed on the troops, which may have included the number of days they could encamp; the use of blank ammunition and times it could be fired; restrictions on digging; and the general maintenance of the common (for example the collection and burial of rubbish). At Lincoln, when a Territorial regiment was quartered in the city it was authorised to train on the South Common in 1916 and 1917 on the understanding that any disturbance to the ground would be repaired on departure. Another example is Wimbledon where restrictions included a requirement to give two days' notice to the Conservators of impending training as well as restrictions on horses and artillery, which were not allowed on cricket pitches, golf courses, in young plantations or on pond dams (TNA: WO 32/18451).

The Pitchcroft, Worcester, was used extensively by the yeomanry in the 19th century and an agreement between the military authorities and the town council allowed for 12 days training a year. This agreement not only placed restrictions on the local community's use and access to the common, but also the aesthetics of the place. In 1903, 103 elms, limes, and horse-chestnuts were planted, but none could be planted in the centre because it was felt that it would impede military activity. The yeomanry also purchased substantial parts of Moorsfields (which was adjacent to and contiguous with the Pitchcroft), with the intention of making about 100 acres of land available for training. Further restrictions and exclusions for the local population were introduced at the beginning of the First World War, when the yeomanry

constructed wooden stable blocks for their horses on the common. Cavalry training was also undertaken on a small part of Hob Moor, York, from 1912–20, for which the local corporation received compensation for 'loss and damage due to the military occupation of land on Hob Moor' (Smith 2004, 61).

Rifle ranges

Small-arms training – the art of weapon handling and firing – was fundamental to any soldier's training and several rifle ranges were established on urban commons to practise marksmanship skills. Many ranges were constructed for the militia and volunteer forces, their location invariably recorded on the Ordnance Survey 1st-edition maps. On Abingdon Common, for example, a rifle range was laid out across the racecourse sometime in the late 18th or early 19th century with the furthest firing point near the grandstand; at Beverley a range was established on Figham Common in 1872 (Pollington and Pearson 2004, 18). At this time, the common was relatively open, which enabled targets to be set up at 50 and 100 yard intervals, out to a distance of 700 yards.

The best examples identified during the course of this project are those on Lincoln's South Common, which probably had their origins in the mid-18th century (perhaps highlighted by a more macabre incident in 1741 when a deserter was sentenced to be shot here (Lincolnshire Archives: Sibthorp Scrapbook, 46)). The surviving butts, which are of 19th- and 20th-century date, provide some of the more dramatic earthworks on the common (see Fig 2.7). Each comprises a steep earthen embayment, at the base of which targets would be placed; they were positioned in such a way as to allow shooting from various distances. The butt bays are cut into the escarpment terrace and utilise former quarries. They vary in width from 12m to 25m across the bay and stand 2m or 3m in height. One of the butts is much smaller than the others and may have been used for small calibre practice (such as pistols or, less likely since there is no covering bank, grenades). It is fully enclosed, the embayment reaching 2m in height and 16m wide at the base, providing one side of a rectangular area 50m in length with the ground within lowered by 1m.

In 1859 South Common was regarded as the most appropriate rifle range for the local volunteers (Lincolnshire Archives: Hill 12) and the local newspapers carried regular commentaries on the competitions held here. However, the needs of the military and those of the public were sometimes at odds; in 1885 trees that had been planted around the ponds were obscuring the line-of-fire as they were reaching maturity and were therefore pruned (Lincolnshire Archives: L1/1/20/1). By 1886 there were three ranges on the common; however, how long they continued in use is unclear, since one of the greatest drawbacks to local recruiting before the First World War was apparently considered to be the lack of a rifle range and it seems likely, therefore, that they had been abandoned in the late 19th or early 20th century.

Practice trenches

Practice trenches – dug mainly during the earlier 20th century (although some may predate this) – are the other main archaeological feature found on the commons. The trenches are quite fragmentary – nowhere do we see the complete systems that are evident, either as earthworks or from aerial photographs, on the major training areas such as Otterburn, Dartmoor and Salisbury Plain, for instance (Charlton and Day 1977, 137; Francis 2002; McOmish *et al* 2002, 138–44; Brown and Field 2007). Only lines of what appear to be firing trenches have been discovered on most town commons, with few traces of communication trenches, shelter bays and the other elements of a fully developed trench system.

Practice trenches were dug on Beverley's Westwood Common; the most noticeable is a small crenellated system, but additionally there are several two-man battle trenches, which probably date to the Second World War. Traces of a single line of military trenching are also evident on Lincoln's South Common (*see* Fig 2.7). It survives as a backfilled trench, crenellated in typical First World War manner and measuring about 1m in width and little more than 0.2m deep. The most prominent portion incorporates five crenellations stretching over 90m, but fragments of the system can be traced for at least 150m. No communication or reserve trenches are evident, but shallow traces of a second line of trenching occur on the lower ground and it may be that these opposing trenches formed part of a set-piece manoeuvre. Some of these trenches may also be related to the tank experiments that were carried out here in 1915 (*see* Fig 5.8).

On Walmgate Stray in York, the most prominent earthworks are the remains of military trenches. They comprise four lengths of crenellated firing trenches with further zigzag trenches that were probably support trenches (Pollington 2004, 16; Fig 5.4). Other examples of the zigzag type of trench are on Newcastle Town Moor; they survive as very slight ditches measuring no more than 20m in length and 0.7m wide (Lofthouse 1995, 37–8; NMR: NZ 26 NW 30).

Manoeuvres and other exercises

Other forms of training took place on the commons but, by their very nature, have left little or no archaeological evidence. This included bayonet practice and field-craft exercises such as patrolling and, as on Beverley's commons, large-scale manoeuvres (Fig 5.5).

Figure 5.4
The shallow remains of First World War practice trenches on Walmgate Stray, York, highlighted by flood water in March 2006.

Figure 5.5
Signalling practice on
Beverley's Westwood
Common in the 19th century
– the windmills were used as
vantage points.

Figure 5.6
Aerial photograph from 1946 of Lincoln's West Common showing the outline of the airfield's circular take-off and landing area and the linear anti-glider ditches. Also visible are ridge-and-furrow, the outline of the racecourse and elements of the golf course.
[RAF/3G/TUD/UK/197 V 5400, 10 May 1946]

Fragments of Mills bombs and grenades, first used in 1915, emphasise the military activity here. A Second World War assault course also survives (apparently uniquely) as earthworks on Walmgate Stray, York (Pollington 2004, 18–20). These somewhat enigmatic earthworks would not have been interpreted correctly but for the oral evidence of local inhabitants.

Commons during wartime

The open spaces beside our towns and cities were also the scene of military activity during wartime from at least the 17th century. During the English Civil War, Scottish troops – who were part of the Parliamentary forces – encamped on Hob Moor, York, in 1644 (Smith 2004, 31) and seven years later the Scottish cavalry of Charles II encamped at the Pitchcroft while awaiting orders prior to the battle of Worcester (Hodgetts 2003, 10). Newcastle upon Tyne, as a result of its geographic position, was strategically placed during the

Anglo-Scottish wars of the 14th century, the English Civil War and the Jacobite Risings in 1715 and 1745. Most of the threats were from the north, making Newcastle Town Moor the obvious place for encampments and mustering. According to the diary of the Methodist preacher, John Wesley, the English mustering army of General Wade had a camp of 15,000 men here prior to the Scottish campaign of 1745 (Charlton 1933, 84). Although these encampments have left no archaeological trace, other English Civil War features have been identified, such as at Oxford's Port Meadow, where a shallow right-angled bank has been interpreted as part of a siege work (Connor 2003, 85).

Early military aviation

During the First World War the use of urban commons by the military was widespread. At Lincoln, for example, an airfield was built on West Common and it was here that the aircraft that had been manufactured in local factories were assembled, tested and dispatched to their

squadrons. In 1917 Lincoln was one of eight towns and cities in England with Acceptance Parks and this particular park had an average output of 25 machines per week at this time (TNA: AIR 1/679/21/13/2203). The airfield – known as No. 4 Aircraft Acceptance Park – was in operation from 1915 until 1919. It comprised two turf landing strips and a landing circle, which was bordered with lime. There were also aircraft hangers and accommodation for the service personnel; the racecourse buildings were also used for accommodation (Walls and Parker 2000, 75–6; Fig 5.6). Little survives of the airfield complex apart from the earthworks of the hanger stances and buildings overlying ridge-and-furrow cultivation.

Other commons were used as military airfields both before and during the First World War. These include Portholme Meadow in Huntingdon, where Blériot aeroplanes were constructed and tested by a local company, Portholme Aerodrome Ltd, in the early 1900s (*see* p 75); the Royal Flying Corps also had a training camp here during the First World War (Poppy *et al* 2006, 188). On the racecourse on Beverley's Westwood Common, an airfield was established to help counter the growing threat from German Zeppelin airships. The paucity of the earthwork remains within the racecourse, when compared to the rest of the common, perhaps indicates that the area was levelled at this time for the airstrip. A 1917 aerial photograph shows that the racecourse track was removed and there were some buildings that may have been related to the airfield (Pearson and Pollington 2004, 39). The racecourse was also used by the military during the Second World War. Port Meadow, Oxford, had a military aerodrome from 1917 to 1922 (McDonald 2007, 90–2).

Town commons were sometimes used in a more ad hoc fashion by early military aviators. In July 1917 ace fighter pilot Gwilym Lewis – then an instructor at the Central Flying School, Upavon – was flying over Marlborough (where he had been a pupil at the college) and he 'perched on the Common for a few minutes' (Lewis 1976, 111).

The Second World War

Evidence of military activity on commons during the Second World War is more widespread and primarily relates to defensive features such as anti-tank and anti-glider obstacles, radar stations, searchlight positions, camps and 'defensive lines'. On Lincoln's West Common, in an area of dense earthworks that represent small-scale quarrying, there are three circular depressions that may have been part of a searchlight position. There are also several linear banks and ditches – characteristic of anti-aircraft ditches (more commonly termed anti-glider ditches) – covering much of the common. As the name implies, they were designed to obstruct enemy aircraft landing. Although the recommended layout was a grid pattern of squares of ditches with spoil heaped along one side, there were variations; in fact none of those identified on commons conformed to this layout. On Lincoln's West Common, for instance, there are five lines of ditches. Each line comprises two rows of interrupted ditches with the upcast piled in the intervening space.

Another good example is on Minchinhampton Common where there are 12 ditches varying in length from 100m to 350m on the level plateau. The ditches average about 3m wide and 0.2m deep with the upcast mounds along one side. An army camp was also established on the edge of the common during the Second World War and additional defences, such as two-man battle trenches (or slit trenches), were also dug on the east side of the common (Smith 2002, 37–8).

Further anti-glider ditches have been identified on Figham Common, Beverley, Biggleswade Common and the Pitchcroft, Worcester. For example, on Figham Common there are three parallel lines of pits, each line consisting of evenly spaced pairs of rectangular pits positioned on either side of a central mound (Pollington and Pearson 2004, 18–19), while at Biggleswade they comprise a series of shallow linear ditches along the eastern side of the common. Also at Biggleswade, the earthwork remains of a searchlight battery comprising a cluster of three platforms and another, possibly generator, position, lie on the eastern side of the common (Fig 5.7). On Port Meadow, Oxford, anti-landing defences were provided by posts with no earthwork component, leaving no visible trace (McDonald 2007,

134). Another form of defence was identified from aerial photographs of Newcastle upon Tyne, which revealed the remnants of a radar station on the northern side of Newcastle Town Moor (NMR: NZ 26 NW 49).

The open landscape of urban commons was also well suited to 'local defence'. At Hungerford pillboxes, road blocks, gun emplacements and a trench were constructed in and around the commons as part of the Kennet and Avon Stop Line during the Second World War (Newsome 2005, 23). Similarly Newcastle Town Moor was part of a northern stop line with pillboxes and tank obstacles, such as concrete blocks placed at specific points across the common (Lofthouse 1995, 36–7). At Abingdon anti-tank obstacles (including a canal) and pillboxes form a defence across the open space beside the town. There are further examples of pillboxes on the commons at Bampton, Godalming and Sudbury.

Temporary defences were also built on the Pitchcroft, Worcester, where old tram tracks were used. In addition, a tree-lined track on the racecourse was used at night as camouflage for petrol tankers; there were also several air-raid shelters and an emergency food centre.

Camps

Urban commons were also used for military camps during the Second World War. The racecourse at York, which is situated on the Knavesmire (and part of Micklegate Stray), was used in this way by 1942 (NMR: SE 54 NE 44).

Newcastle Town Moor was the site of a prisoner-of-war camp in the 1940s. An aerial photograph shows that it covered the eastern half of Nuns Moor and comprised a series of prefabricated buildings enclosed by a perimeter fence. According to local knowledge the camp held Italian POWs. It was demolished in 1959 and the area returned to grassland (NMR: NZ 26 NW 31). Another prisoner-of-war camp was located on Southampton Common and was probably still in use in 1948 (NMR: SU 41 SW 278).

A testing time – the military use of commons for experiments and testing

In industrial towns and cities where military equipment was manufactured, commons provided an ideal testing ground. An early

example is Wimbledon Common, which was the scene for rocket tests by Sir William Congreve in 1808. Several gunnery experiments were carried out at Lydd – these were not without their risks. In 1891, for example, there was a bore premature explosion in a mortar and another two years later in a 5in BL howitzer (TNA: WO 32/9060). Another common that was used for munitions production was Canford Heath, Poole, where part of the land was occupied by the Royal Ordnance Factory (Hoskins and Stamp 1963, 169).

Lincoln's South Common was also host to military experiments when a prototype tank known as 'Little Willie' was tested here during the First World War (Fig 5.8). The undulating terrain across the common was an ideal area to test the tank's capability to negotiate the terrain and cross trenches. When production was

underway in 1917 the War Department applied to fence off about a hectare of land on the common in order to park about 200 tanks. The council acceded, but placed conditions regarding damage; however, much more than the agreed plot was used and the trials evidently destroyed several cricket pitches. After the war the area of the park was reinstated with steam cultivators when it was ploughed and harrowed (Anon 1920, 19; Lincolnshire Archives: L1/ 1/20/9). No physical traces of these historic trials therefore remain.

Town commons during the Cold War

The most significant use of an urban common during the Cold War was that of Newbury's Greenham Common (*see* Fig 8.2), which was

Figure 5.8
The No. 1 Lincoln Machine – or 'Little Willie' tank as it became known – undergoing trials over a trench on South Common, Lincoln, in 1915. [The Tank Museum, Bovington]

initially used as an airfield for American long-range bombers, but latterly as a storage facility for cruise missiles. Even before this Cold War period, Greenham Common had been used extensively by the military. As early as 1740, a map shows a military camp here and, in 1872, 20,000 troops were involved in an exercise on the common. During the First World War it was again used for infantry and armoured exercises, but it was not until 1941 that an airfield was built on Greenham Common and part of Crookham Common. It continued to be used throughout the Second World War, figuring prominently during the preparations for the D-Day landings in 1944 and subsequent operations.

Following the Second World War there was a brief lull in the military use of Greenham Common; however, in response to the growing threat from the Soviet Union, the airfield was re-established and was once more operational in 1954, despite protests from the local population. The common continued to be used as an American facility throughout the later decades of the 20th century. In 1988 it was revealed that the commoners' rights might make building on the base illegal and the Ministry of Defence was partly successful in attempting to pay the commoners to extinguish some of their rights. Two years later, however, the House of Lords ruled that the military by-laws prohibiting trespass on the base were illegal. In 1992 the Americans left the base and the military decided to return both Greenham and Crookham Commons to the inhabitants of Newbury.

At the beginning of the 21st century, the commons were again open to the public, stock fencing erected and grazing reintroduced.

Britain's nuclear policy and the military use of Greenham Common were clearly contentious issues and spawned numerous demonstrations and rallies. The most prominent, and arguably the most significant, was the women's 'peace camp' that was established on the perimeter of the airfield in 1981. The camp itself was, in the main, a rather flimsy array of structures; however, archaeological investigations have revealed a complex arrangement. There is evidence for three camps. The earliest dates from the 1950s and comprised tent 'pads' and hearths. The second camp was the largest and was perhaps divided into three elements – one for occupation while the others were for communal or ceremonial use. The third camp, the most recent, includes a habitation area and symbolic features such as painted fence posts (Schofield *et al* 2003).

Permanent military areas

The earliest common to be acquired permanently by the military was Woolwich Common, which was taken over in the third quarter of the 18th century. Woolwich was a small fishing village until the beginning of the 16th century when the dockyard and the Royal Arsenal were established on the banks of the River Thames. By the end of the 18th century the town was expanding rapidly and developing many urban characteristics. As a consequence the Ordnance

Figure 5.9
This illustration from a map of December 1811 shows military housing on Woolwich Common.
[The National Archives, ref. MPH1/32/2]

Board acquired more land, including the open space on the common, and in 1775 the Royal Artillery and Royal Engineers moved into new barracks on Barrack Field, which lay beside the common (Vincent 1888, 394; Fig 5.9).

Later, in the early 19th century, there were encroachments on some parts of Woolwich Common, which were subsequently purchased, pulled down and the area 'levelled' (ibid, 388, 391). Some of the more prosperous local inhabitants, seeing the advantages (not least in health) of living outside the town with views across the countryside, also built houses along the western fringes of the common (ibid, 394).

Woolwich Common covers an area of about 54 hectares and lies to the north of the town; it is a landscape of gently rising ground, which was ideally suited for military training. Permanent accommodation for soldiers and their families dates to the early 19th century when they were billeted here after the Peace of Amiens in 1802. Many soldiers' families, however, had to live on the western margin of the common in mud huts. These 'miserable hovels' were later demolished and brick cottages built in their place, which continued to be used until 1875 when an outbreak of diphtheria highlighted their insanitary conditions and they too were pulled down (ibid, 397). A map dating to 1863 depicts the soldiers' accommodation, which was a grid pattern of barrack huts and included officers' and senior NCOs' accommodation, a guardroom, a large canteen, a skittle alley and stables for over a thousand horses (TNA: WO 78/2890). The extent of military influence on Woolwich Common is highlighted in the 1881 census, when there were nearly 400 soldiers encamped on the common (Vincent 1888, 467).

Other places where barracks were built on urban commons include Colchester and Newcastle upon Tyne. At Colchester this was precipitated by complaints from innkeepers about the soldiers' behaviour, which led to some common land being surrendered by the burgesses in 1794 for barracks (*VCH Essex IX* 1994, 258). At Newcastle Town Moor barracks were built in 1830 and by the end of the century they had expanded and included separate buildings for the infantry and artillery (Soc of Antiq Newcastle: PM32, Oliver 1852).

An artillery training area was established on Okehampton Common in the late 19th century, which was to become one of the main training areas in the United Kingdom. Initially, the training season lasted for only five months of the year – from May to September – and the commoners were compensated for the loss of their rights during this period. Later Okehampton became a permanent facility and as such over 100 years of military activity can be seen on the former common. Amongst the earliest features is the hutted camp, which dates to the late 19th century, as well as the remains of a former artillery target railway and a trench system (NMR: SX 59 SE 139). Part of the West Ripe at Lydd, which was one of two commons that bordered the southern side of the town, was also permanently acquired by the military. The eastern part of West Ripe is now a small park surrounded by housing, but the western part was acquired by the military in 1883 and used for training and testing, with accommodation for permanent and visiting troops.

6

A social dimension to town commons

Since the early 17th century many town commons have been transformed into places of leisure and recreation, places where people come to see and be seen. They were (and still are) places of assembly for more organised events such as fairs, agricultural shows, political gatherings and celebrations (Fig 6.1). It was, however, the 18th and 19th centuries that witnessed more widespread changes – particularly following enclosure – by the creation of 'people's parks' with lakes, wide tree-lined avenues and scattered clumps of trees. In addition organised sporting activities increased dramatically in this period leading, in some instances, to restrictions in access; nevertheless, the changes reflected a perceived social need.

Some events – the fairs, the agricultural shows and assemblies – leave little or no archaeological evidence apart, perhaps, from the opportune aerial photograph that reveals the tell-tale signs of tents and show grounds; it is largely the local newspapers, posters and maps that record such events. Although they are all but archaeologically invisible they are nevertheless important events in the social life of any town or city.

The increasing urbanisation of towns and cities during the later 19th century inevitably led to pressures on land and commons were a prime target for encroachment and development. This could happen in a piecemeal manner or even a more wholesale fashion

Figure 6.1
A bonfire of the Great Torrington Cavaliers' model of HMS Victory *on Great Torrington Common, 2005. [Photograph courtesy of the Great Torrington Cavaliers]*

where much of the common was taken in. Piecemeal encroachments in this context include the building of hospitals, workhouses, cemeteries and mortuary chapels on common land either beside the town or in an isolated position well away from habitation. An example is Newcastle upon Tyne where, by 1830, barracks, a hospital and garden allotments had encroached on part of Castle Leazes beyond the bounds of the city. In some cases the former extent of a common can be seen in the street layout. Nottingham is a well-documented example where some of the former open-field furlongs are fossilised in the street pattern and the principal routes follow tracks and paths across the common (eg Carter 1983; Hoskins 1988, 224–8), but it is a process that was witnessed elsewhere in the country. At Grimsby, where the medieval town clustered around the parish church with its two commons – East Marsh and West Marsh – lying between the town and the Humber, a strip of land was leased in the early 19th century in East Marsh for a ropery with a flax-spinning mill close-by. However, it was the coming of the railway and the building of a new dock later in the century that heralded a dramatic increase in the town's population that caused the housing development on the East Marsh (Gillett 1970, 213).

Paradoxically, the changes and pressures on urban commons were therefore twofold. On the one hand there was a clear need and desire to use them for the common good and well-being of the local community by providing places for exercise and recreation, while at the same time they were seen as places that could be exploited and developed for an ever-increasing population and urban infrastructure. This chapter explores the changes and developments on urban commons from a place of agricultural and industrial exploitation to one where leisure and recreation were the overriding interests, but where there were also constant pressures on the limited land resources leading, in some cases, to the partial or complete loss of a common.

Commons as places of recreation

'Improved commons'

Despite several urban commons being converted into 'people's parks', the change was by no means universal and many have retained their 'wilderness' and open space characteristics. In some cases there appears to have been

little enthusiasm for a park, as in the case of Doncaster where the common had been used for recreation for generations. In 1887 it was suggested that the queen's jubilee should be marked by creating a public park, but as reported on 7 January of that year, 'we have the Common and Hexthorpe Flatts for recreation' (*Doncaster Gazette*, 7 Jan 1887).

Recreation on commons was clearly an important aspect of the social life of the townsfolk. Walking on Beverley's Westwood Common, for example, was an acknowledged 'pleasure' and in the 1780s a formal promenade, the New Walk, was created when the corporation agreed to subscribe £20 as soon as the 'gentlemen and ladies' contributed £30 (*VCH Yorks VI* 1989, 132). Improvements for recreation have also been recognised from English Heritage's earthwork survey on Lincoln's South Common where part of a terraced walk along the north-facing escarpment survives. The walk, which was called 'The Promenade', was constructed in 1844. Trees were planted and railings installed along its course. Two ponds were created out of a disused quarry and trees planted on the flatter ground and, later, over 200 seats were placed in various places around the common (Field 2005, 64). In contrast, no formal walks were constructed on Lincoln's West Common, presumably because of the prevalence of sports fields and horse-racing here; however, several plantations and the 'Jubilee Pond' were constructed in the late 19th century and the 20th century to break up what would otherwise be a rather mundane and monotonous landscape.

Analysis of maps and paintings can also illustrate the changing nature of urban commons. A painting dating from before the walks were laid out in 'The Quarry', Shrewsbury, in 1719 shows the area when it was used principally for pasturing cattle, with what appears to be a boatyard on the river bank. Forty years later the landscape had been transformed – gone were the cows and in their place an avenue of trees linked the town to the river's edge, with further tree planting elsewhere on the common. Southampton Common provides another example – here there are several features dating to at least the mid-19th century (including the site of a former gallows). From two entrances along the eastern side of the common, a carriage drive meandered around the perimeter. The date of this drive is unclear, but it had gone out of use by the late 19th century since it was cut to the north by a straight, tree-lined avenue and what was termed a 'new reservoir', while to the south two horse racecourses overlay the carriageway. Clumps of trees and bushes punctuate the landscape, breaking up this wide open expanse of land.

On some commons there was a clear delineation for specific pursuits. The part of Petersfield Heath Common that was closest to the town was specifically set aside as a recreation ground and golf course, and a pavilion was built sometime between 1843 and 1891. Nearby, a large pond that had been constructed in 1741 (Tavener 1957, 65–6) adds to the aesthetic value of the area (*see* Fig 1.3). Beyond the recreation ground, however, in a position furthest from the town, an isolation hospital was built at the end of the 19th century. Similarly at Northampton, pleasure walks were laid out on Cow Meadow in 1703 and £30 was spent on planting trees; however, in 1870 a cattle market

was built on part of the common leaving the remainder for recreation (*VCH Northants III* 1930, 22–3). At Saffron Walden the eastern side of the common is the focus of a turf maze (Fig 6.2). This labyrinth, which dates to at least 1699, is about 35m in diameter and approximately 1,500m long; its circuitous route to the centre presumably provides much entertainment (as well as a little exercise). In the centre is a raised mound, which had an ash tree on top until it was burnt down during a Guy Fawkes' celebration in 1823.

Despite giving a feeling of freedom and enjoyment, other restrictions were often placed on the use of commons, particularly 'public' rights as opposed to commoners' rights. At Tewkesbury, despite the activities on the Severn Ham described by John Moore, there are no public rights across the open ground apart from a single 'right-of-way', nor is it permitted to moor boats along the river bank.

Parks and arboretums

The earliest recorded public park on an urban common is at Moorfields, London, where the moor was filled in and the ground level raised and converted to a public park in the autumn of 1607. It initially consisted of two walks, bordered by walls and trees, that crossed centrally and where people could 'take the ayre' (Lambert 1921, 87). It was, however, during the 18th century that several commons were converted to public parks and arboretums. Examples include the commons at Bath, Bournemouth and Bradford, along with Norwich's Chapel Fields (Girouard 1990, 117–54). In Grimsby a public park was proposed for the West Marsh in the 1870s and a few years later a public promenade was constructed along the River Freshney and planted with trees; another small park, the Duke of York's Gardens, was also created elsewhere on West Marsh (Gillett 1970, 239).

Several arboretums were created on urban commons in the 19th century, two examples being Nottingham and Lincoln. Following the enclosing of Nottingham's open fields and meadows in 1845, several open spaces were specifically set aside for recreation – one of these was to become the arboretum. It was created by the horticultural publicist Samuel Curtis in 1850 and opened to the public in 1852. The park was a place for leisure and relaxation in a garden setting, as well as providing some education and encouraging people to

Figure 6.2
Richard Gough's 1768 plan of the turf maze at Saffron Walden.
[Bodleian Library, University of Oxford, Gough Maps 8, fol 6b, item a]

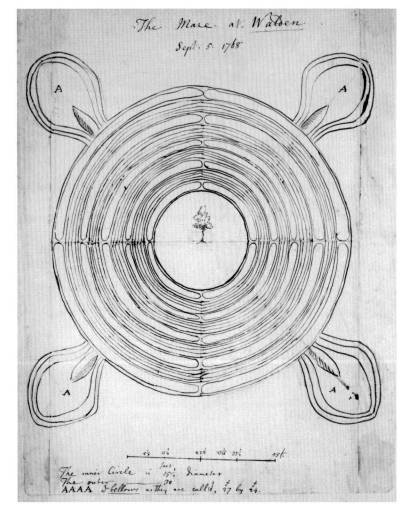

take more notice of their surroundings. From the main entrance lodge, the principal route was along the spine of the park with several interconnecting walks to other 'social areas'. There was also a perimeter path backing onto the plantings that encircled the whole site. Features within the arboretum include a lake, bandstand, drinking fountain, refreshment rooms and aviaries; in 1857 a pagoda was erected that contained a bell taken from a temple in Canton during the Opium Wars (NMR: SK 54 SE 56; Fig 6.3). Trees and shrubs were judicially planted throughout, with their botanical names affixed onto small enamel labels. The undulating grassland was levelled in places for dancing. The park drew a large number of visitors from the surrounding area and further afield. Initially, the arboretum was only open three days a week and a small entrance fee was charged; however, following objections the fee was abolished. People clearly had vivid memories of their times in the park, even when they were in a totally alien environment. On one occasion during the First World War, for example, a local soldier on the Western Front prosaically likened the night scene before him to 'an arboretum flower show firework display' (Nottinghamshire Archives: DD/2402/1/3).

An arboretum was also created on the steep escarpment of Monk's Leys Common in Lincoln 20 years after the one at Nottingham. Although Monk's Leys was clearly a valuable pasture during the medieval and post-medieval periods, its importance had waned by the mid-19th century and was a cause of concern and friction amongst the townspeople. In 1856 it was described as:

…an oblong piece of ground occupying the hill-side. It is exclusively set apart for the dispasturage of the stock of the Freemen of the city; but most probably the time is not far distant when the municipality will be rescued from the odium of preserving large tracts of commonable land which do no good, and are a premium for idleness, drunkenness, and perjury among the lower classes.

(Lincoln Reference Library: Abell Collection, *Agriculture & Commons* **1**, 84b)

In 1870 a proposal for a park to 'keep the city's men out of public houses and in the open air with their families' (ibid) was sanctioned and Edward Milner, a leading landscape gardener, was asked to draw up a design. The arboretum was ideally situated close to the city centre and provided panoramic views over

the countryside. It was opened in 1872, attracting an estimated 25,000 people. Several events were organised for the opening including band concerts, a firework display and a balloon ascent.

The 12-acre site (similar in size to Derby Arboretum (Elliott 2000) but smaller than the one at Nottingham) was elaborately laid out, with a long terrace on the upper slope, which was in effect a grand promenade bordered by an avenue of trees and a fountain at either end. The terrace was approached from the lower levels by three flights of steps, one on either end and one in the centre. On the lower level there was a yew maze and shrubs, a pavilion, an

Figure 6.3
The spoils of war and symbols of patriotism. Housed within the pagoda at Nottingham Arboretum is a replica of a Chinese bell that was taken by soldiers of the 59th Regiment of Foot from a temple in the city of Canton during the Opium Wars. At the base of the pagoda are Russian cannon that were captured in 1857 during the siege of Sebastopol.

ornamental lake with rustic grottoes and aquatic plants, a swan house with a thatched roof, statues and monuments elsewhere. At one of the entrances there was a tearoom with seating for some 200 people. Twelve years after the opening, a permanent bandstand was installed and there was a proposal to erect a 'more suitable and commodious arbour or summer house in lieu of the existing one' (Minutes of Arboretum Committee 20 Nov 1883–24 Feb 1890).

The arboretum at Monk's Leys Common, Lincoln, was a tremendous success (although no games of football were allowed!). Local organisations, as well as others from further afield, regularly applied to hold galas, fêtes and dances. Band concerts were extremely popular throughout the summer months. In 1888 there was a programme of 'promenade concerts' with military and civilian bands. Although many

of the bands were local, others travelled considerable distances to perform (a 30-strong Royal Engineers band travelled by train from Chatham and a Royal Marine band from Colchester). The following year there were 18 concerts, which were attended by nearly 41,000 people. Firework displays usually concluded the season when the grounds were illuminated with 4,000 lamps and 250 lanterns. The concerts appear to have been so successful that in 1890 it was resolved that businesses in the city should close on Wednesday afternoons during the summer so that people could attend. Although entry to the arboretum was normally free, the summer season of band concerts were ticket events.

'Taking the waters' – the use of commons as spas

The reputation of some commons was enhanced by their proximity to mineral springs, and the growing popularity of 'taking the waters' for their medicinal qualities from the early 17th century led to some villages expanding into urban centres in their own right. Harrogate provides a good example of the popularity of the springs encouraging urbanisation. Prior to the enclosure of the Forest of Knaresborough, Harrogate consisted of two villages, High and Low Harrogate; it was a place that was renowned for its springs of medicinal water, discovered here in the later 16th century (commonly called Harrogate Spas). Where the springs were found on the common wasteland, and as long as the forest remained unenclosed, the public had access across the common to drink from the springs. With the enclosure of the Forest of Knaresborough in the 1770s, steps were taken to preserve and protect this resource and 200 acres were converted into common pasture. Harrogate Stray became a place where people could take air and exercise after taking the waters (Hargrove 1809, 113; Haythornthwaite 1959; Walker nd).

Another example is Tunbridge Wells, where the spa town developed close to a mineral, or chalybeate, spring in the early 17th century. The apparent health properties of the spring water, which was sited on common land in the manor of Rusthall, ensured its popularity. In 1608 the first well was dug for the growing number of visitors and further improvements were made in 1664, including a new enclosure with an ornamental arch (Fig 6.4). In 1682 an agreement was reached between the lord of the

Figure 6.4
An engraving by S Clark, dating to 1664, of people taking the waters from the chalybeate spring at Tunbridge Wells. [Image courtesy of Tunbridge Wells Museum & Art Gallery]

manor and the freeholders allowing the building of shops and lodging facilities for visitors on part of the common beside the spring (later known as The Pantiles); in addition, the freeholders were compensated for loss of grazing rights. The rights of the freeholders were later formalised in the Rusthall Manor Act of 1739. Another cold bath and pleasure grounds (comprising an ornamental pavilion surrounded by gardens with lakes, watercourses and fountains) were established on nearby Rusthall Common in 1708; however, by 1766 the bath was no longer in use.

Spas were also created on the commons of 'historic' towns. On the northern side of Swine Moor, Beverley, a well was dug for bathing and drinking in 1684. In 1747 the existing building was replaced by a new one and the spa leased to a tenant. By 1816 it seems that the spa was no longer in use (*VCH Yorks VI* 1989, 239); however, although it may have fallen into some disrepair, it appears that it was still functioning until the middle of the 19th century when it was '…used only as a bath possessing the property of extreme coldness' (Sheahan and Whellan 1856, 295). The spa continued to be shown on maps until the 1956 Ordnance Survey map, which marks it as Swinemoor Wells and still depicts part of the spa's structure (OS 1956 map, 1:10,560); however, by the end of the decade these had finally been demolished and by the 1960s it was only marked as a small wooded enclosure (OS 1972 map, 1:2500), as it remains today.

In the early 18th century there was an attempt to make Northampton a fashionable place to 'take the waters' following the discovery of a chalybeate spring (known as the Vigo Well) on the Cow Meadow. In 1784 a new walk was laid out between Vigo Well and St Thomas's Well and planted with trees 'to form an agreeable shelter' (*VCH Northants III* 1930, 23 and map facing 30) with a fence to prevent the cows accessing the spring.

Agricultural shows

The large, uninterrupted space on urban commons also provided the ideal setting for agricultural shows, which became increasingly popular during the second half of the 19th century following the formation of the county agricultural societies (although some shows pre-dated the societies). These events were of great economic importance to a town and provided a venue for rural and urban communities to meet; places where livestock could be exhibited; and places where new agricultural implements could be displayed and demonstrated. Agricultural shows took place on several urban commons, such as Newcastle Town Moor, Tewkesbury's Severn Ham, Marlborough Common and Lincoln's South and West Commons. These events were important social occasions; for example, on Tewkesbury's Severn Ham in 1863, as well as the cattle show there was a flower show, a regatta on the River Severn, an athletic competition and band concerts (Fig 6.5).

Figure 6.5
Tewkesbury Agricultural Show on the Severn Ham in 1863.
[Museum of English Rural Life, University of Reading]

In 1854 a Royal Agricultural Show was held on South Common, Lincoln, where ranks of temporary buildings and fenced enclosures for the animals were erected. Fifteen years later, following the formation of the Lincolnshire Agricultural Society, the first county show was held on South Common (however, subsequent shows were either held on West Common or elsewhere in the county (Ruddock 1983; Walker 2004)). The organising committee made efforts to involve the local community by encouraging tradesmen to decorate their premises in celebration of the show. Besides the livestock competitions there was also prize money for various farmworkers such as foremen, shepherds, labourers and head waggoners, 'so long as they had good character for sobriety or did not return drunk with their horses' (Ruddock 1983, 49). Although these shows were popular (in the closing decade of the 19th century and the first two decades of the 20th, for example, attendance was between 20,000 and 30,000 people), there appears initially to have been an attempt to minimise contact between the social classes, which manifested itself in a number of ways, such as the seating arrangements and provision of refreshment stands (the latter were separated between first- and second-class facilities). However, a more effective and overtly social segregation was in the ticketing policy, where a varied pricing policy was instigated and during the 1880s the last day was referred to as the 'people's day' when the entrance fee was lowered (Walker 2004).

Commons as 'places of isolation'

A recurring theme is the prevalence of workhouses, isolation hospitals, prisons, cemeteries and mortuary chapels on commons; indeed, the presence of any of these, or a barracks, in a modern town may be the best clue as to the location of former common land. Many of these institutions date to the late 19th century, although there are earlier examples, such as St Leonard's leper hospital at Sudbury, which was built in the 14th century and later used for the aged and infirm. The hospital, which was not suppressed at the Dissolution, lay about a mile to the north of the town on the boundary of what later became known as North Meadow Common (OS 1st-edition map 1886; Hodson 1891, 268–74; NMR: TL 84 SE 9). Nothing survives of this building. Another example is the two-storey lunatic asylum that was built on the northern edge of Chapel Fields, Norwich, in 1712 (NMR: TG 20 NW 378).

There appears to have been a conscious effort, where possible, to build some isolation hospitals well away from habitation, such as the smallpox hospital on Lincoln's West Common and the isolation hospital built in 1899 at Petersfield, which comprised a ward, administrative block and laundry (NMR: SU 72 SE 39). At Newcastle upon Tyne, two hospitals were built on the Town Moor. One was built in 1893 on the southern side of the common near the barracks as 'a home for incurables'; it comprised a central administrative block and pavilion wards (NMR: NZ 26 NW 36). To the north there was a smallpox isolation hospital and mortuary, both demolished by 1959 (Lofthouse 1995, 50; NMR: NZ 26 NW 33).

Workhouses – possibly because of the social stigma or simply because of lack of space elsewhere – were also built on commons. For example, one was built on Huntingdon's Walnut Tree Common in 1836–7. Its design was based on the '200-pauper plan', which had been published by the Poor Law Commissioners in 1835. By the end of the 19th century it had been converted into an infirmary. Cemeteries were also laid out on urban commons due to a lack of space; some were quite elaborately designed, such as the cemetery at the Cow Paddle in Lincoln, which was extended by the end of the 19th century when a 'grid' pattern cemetery was established with a mortuary chapel and a walk in the shape of a wheel with sinuous spokes (Fig 6.6). Cemeteries are also seen just outside Westwood and Hurn Commons, Beverley, and at Woolwich, Wandsworth, Hammersmith, Eltham and Southampton Commons, while part of the Pitchcroft, Worcester, is known as the 'Jewish Cemetery'.

Since many urban commons became renowned as places where discontented townspeople might gather (see pp 73–4), it was no accident that they were often chosen as the sites for penal institutions and gallows. For example Donkey's Common, Cambridge – enclosed in 1811 and now a sports complex – was the site of the town's gaol from 1827 to 1878. Wormwood Scrubs Prison in Lambeth, London, was also built on common land in the 1880s using prisoner labour. The west side of York's Knavesmire, opposite Hob Moor, was the site of a gallows named the York 'Tyburn', presumably in imitation of the famous London

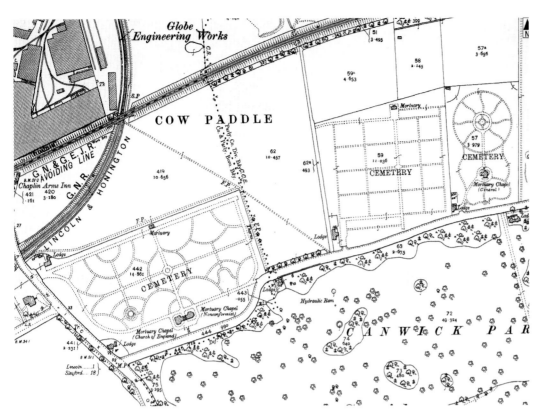

Figure 6.6
During the 19th century an elaborate cemetery, in many ways resembling a formal garden, was laid out in the south-western corner of the Cow Paddle, Lincoln. [Reproduced from the 1889 Ordnance Survey map, 1:2500]

gallows of that name. Crowds flocked to see the spectacle of executions there from the early 16th century onwards, including the execution of the most notorious highwayman, Dick Turpin, in 1739. The last execution on the Knavesmire took place in 1801 and the gallows was removed in 1812 (*VCH York* 1961, 247, 497). Southampton Common was also the site of a gallows. Executions were carried out on Brandon Hill, Bristol, which was a haunt of highwaymen and thieves. Gallows also stood on the southern part of Kennington Common, where a church was erected in 1822.

Commons for sports

Urban commons have been used by townspeople for sports of all kinds for many centuries, although it was not until the later 19th century that permanent pitches and grounds were established. Major sporting 'spectacles', such as prize fights and horse races, are covered in the following chapter.

Cricket was one of the earliest recorded sports being played on an urban common. The first reference to the game was in the mid-16th century at Guildford when John Derrick testified that he 'and diverse of his fellows did runne

and play there at creckett and other plaies' (Altham 1962, 21–9). By the beginning of the 18th century, the sport was becoming increasingly popular and played on several commons in and around London. Clapham Common was the scene for one of a series of five games played in March 1700 'for £10 a head each game and £20 the odd one' (ibid, 23). Cricket rapidly became a spectator sport and wagers were made as to the outcome. Frequently these early games degenerated into disorder, presumably, in part, caused by irate punters. A match on Chelsea Common in 1731 ended in a fight amongst the spectators; six years later another incident occurred, this time on Kennington Common, that resulted in a woman having her leg broken whereupon the Prince of Wales, who was attending the game, 'was pleased to order her ten guineas' (ibid, 36).

Cricket was also played on urban commons throughout the country, particularly from the mid-18th century – examples include Marlborough Common where it was played in 1787; Lincoln's West Common in 1834; Southampton Common by 1843; and on Grimsby's East Marsh. These early games were not without conflicts with other users of the commons; on East Marsh, for example, there was a dispute in 1823 between the cricketers and the freemen since the freemen's stock were being injured (Fig 6.7) and all ball games were forbidden. It was not until 1844 that the cricket club was eventually given permission to play there again (Gillett 1970, 185).

Football was another popular team sport played on urban commons. The Marlborough Town Football Club, for example, played regularly on its common from 1871 until 1937 when they moved elsewhere (*VCH Wilts XII* 1983, 210). Football pitches were not static, particularly on those commons that have been levelled or where the ground was already reasonably level. On Lincoln's West Common, for example, although there are currently six pitches, their number and location have varied over the years.

Sports such as bear- and bull-baiting and cock-fighting also took place. On Westwood Common, Beverley, the remains of a bull-baiting ring marked on the Ordnance Survey 1st-edition 25in map (1855) can still be seen as a circular depression, 12m in diameter, in a

level area in between two quarry hollows (Fig 6.8a). A metal ring securely embedded at the centre of the depression was used for tethering the bull (Fig 6.8b). Some 2m away from the ring is a track eroded by the tethered animal circling around the bottom of the pit. The pit is overlooked from above and there is some evidence to suggest that there was seating. Bull-baiting on Westwood Common was banned by the town corporation in 1824 (Pearson and Pollington 2004, 45–6).

The sport that has arguably made the greatest impact on the commons is golf, since the courses are almost ubiquitous and cover such large areas. Although its origins were in Scotland, it was being played on Blackheath Common in London in the mid-18th century and later on other London commons such as Clapham Common and Wimbledon Common. The formation of a club on Wimbledon Common illustrates the process that was probably replicated on many other commons following enclosure. In 1865 some members of

Figure 6.7
Cricket and cows – an example of the conflicting interests of sport and the more traditional grazing rights on commons during the 19th century.

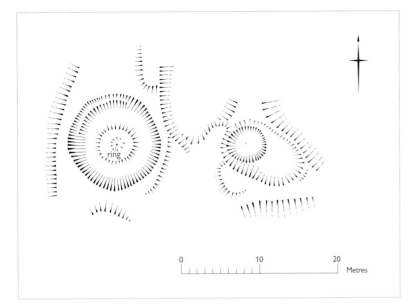

the London Scottish Rifle Volunteers, who were posted nearby, met on the common to form the London Scottish Golf Club. The manorial rights over the common were held by the 5th Earl Spencer, who gave permission for the course to be laid out. Later, in 1871, the manorial rights were transferred by Act of Parliament to a Board of Conservators elected by the rate-payers; it was this body that became responsible for the management of Wimbledon Common and its use for the playing of games (including golf).

Elsewhere in the country, courses were also laid out on commons, particularly during the 1880s and 1890s (although a course was established at Manchester in 1818 on Kersal Moor (Browning 1955, 90)); these included Minchinhampton (*see* Fig 2.4), Marlborough, Lincoln and Beverley's Westwood Common. The course on Lincoln's West Common was established in 1890 and was the earliest in Lincolnshire (there was another course on South Common prior to the turn of the century, but by 1913 problems with animals led to an application to enclose some of the greens).

These early courses, however, were not the managed greens that are so familiar today, but were sometimes quite rough with such natural hazards as ditches and gorse to take the place of bunkers and, in the words of Browning, '… the links received no attention; the only green-keepers were the rabbits' (1955, 165). As late as 1927 he recollects having to contend with numerous obstacles such as cyclists, grazing animals, lamp-posts and rows of washing

fluttering on lines on Malvern Common's golf course (ibid, 167).

Golf courses are occasionally upgraded, new greens and bunkers built, ponds created and trees planted, all of which result in an ever-changing landscape. The earthwork remains of former bunkers and tees also add to the fabric of a golf course and chart its evolution. As well as natural and artificial obstacles, archaeo-logical monuments are also incorporated into a course design. This is apparent on Petersfield Heath Common where the golf course lies amongst the Bronze Age barrow cemetery with a golf pavilion positioned almost in the centre of the common. Similarly on Minchinhampton Common, a 'green' was laid out along the rear of the Amberley Cross Bank.

As well as these games being played on the wide open spaces on the commons, others, such as bowls and tennis were confined within much smaller courts and greens. Bowls – which reached its peak of popularity during the 17th and early 18th century (Borsay 1989, 175) – was played on greens on several town commons including Looe, Great Torrington and Lincoln.

Bathing was also a popular pursuit on commons, especially where they lay beside rivers. At the Pitchcroft and Moorsfields in Worcester, the corporation moored bathing barges on the River Severn beside the common. In 1928 bathing was restricted to two barges and the portion of the river immediately west of them where the bathers would be screened from sensitive eyes by industrial premises. In

Figure 6.8a (above, left) English Heritage's survey of earthworks of a former bull-baiting ring on Westwood Common, Beverley; the slight ledge on the north-west side of the pit could indicate the presence of seating. After bull-baiting was banned in 1824 the pit may have continued in use for tethering livestock. The second pit, to the east, may have been another bull-baiting ring or possibly a cockpit.

Figure 6.8b (above, right) The iron ring (approx 200mm in diameter) for tethering the bull still remains in the centre of the main earthwork circle.

Figure 6.9
Ice skating on the frozen
Port Meadow, Oxford, at the
turn of the 20th century.
[NMR CC73/00049]

1874 a swimming pool had been constructed in the centre of the common; it closed in 1884 when the town decided to build a new pool in a more convenient site close to the town centre (*VCH Worcs III* 1913, 229). However, the pool is marked on the 1893 Ordnance Survey map (OS 1893 map, 1:2500). On Lincoln's West Common a small concrete pool was constructed in the early 20th century and appears to have been in use until at least the middle of the century. Although disused and heavily overgrown, it is now a sanctuary for wildlife and the occasional stray golf ball.

Extreme weather conditions also provided welcome recreational opportunities for town dwellers. In the winter Kelsey's Pond, the old clay pit on York's Hob Moor, used to freeze and townspeople would skate on it. In one year the ice was thick enough for a hundred people to skate and a wind-up gramophone provided musical accompaniment. Ice skating was popular on Port Meadow, Oxford (Fig 6.9), where boats were also sailed during floods in 1875. On Portholme Meadow, Huntingdon, flooding often coincided with severe frosts and the meadow became a huge ice rink, where a version of ice hockey known as 'Bandy' was born (Hull 1999).

7

High days and holidays

For the vast majority of people in English towns working hours were long and until recent times, with the exception of public holidays and Sundays, there was little break from daily labour. Opportunities to travel far from home were also very limited, since travel was difficult and time-consuming before turnpike roads and railways were built. Even when these forms of transport became available an annual outing to the seaside or other attraction by train or charabanc was the highlight of the year for most people. Relief from toil was sought and provided closer to home in the form of travelling fairs and shows or festivals held throughout the year, particularly on important dates in the town calendar. Special events such as royal jubilees and coronations or the ends of wars were all celebrated, while the popular imagination was excited by one-off spectacles, often of a sporting or religious nature.

Regular events

From at least the 19th century, town commons provided the venue for carnivals and processions. Stafford's annual Pageant procession, for example, led to the common, where there would be a fair, jazz bands and dances. During the 19th century regattas and water carnivals were also popular events on riverside urban commons. Tewkesbury's Severn Ham held its first in 1860, while another was held at Worcester's Pitchcroft, where rowing races and associated amusements also took place from at least 1790 (Fig 7.1).

Urban commons have long been the site for town firework displays, which needed to be kept well away from urban buildings. Displays on the Severn Ham took place on Bonfire Night during the 19th century and as part of coronation celebrations in 1902 (Pain 1992, 59, 84–5).

Figure 7.1
Worcester's Pitchcroft was the venue for many attractions. This scene is of a carnival between the wars.
[From the collection of Mr Ron Shuard]

Figure 7.2
Firework display on
Midsummer Common,
Cambridge, in 2007.
[NMR DP070679]

On Midsummer Common, Cambridge, a large annual display held by the city council still attracts 30,000 spectators (Fig 7.2). And at Great Torrington the Cavaliers build a large combustible structure annually and set it alight on part of the 365-acre common (*see* Fig 6.1).

Touring shows

Touring shows, fairs and circuses are still a frequent sight on urban commons. In Stafford, for example, during the first half of the 20th century a large fair visited the common at least twice a year, one visit coinciding with the town's annual Pageant (Fig 7.3). Touring circuses also visited urban commons regularly. Bertram Mills, Billy Smart and Chippendale Circuses – with performers including Coco the Clown and wire-walkers – all appeared on Stafford Common. Bizarre attractions were also seen, such as Mary Ann Bevan, 'the world's ugliest woman', who appeared at the Knavesmire, York, in 1928 (*York Herald* 1928, 1) and the 'Giraffe-Necked Woman' who appeared on Stafford Common in the 1930s (Mrs M Bolton, *pers comm*).

More unusual touring shows drew large numbers of townspeople and became the talk of the day. One such popular attraction was Buffalo Bill's Wild West Show, run by William F Cody, one of the greatest showmen of the 19th century (Fig 7.4). The show visited Britain in 1887 and was such a success that it toured the country in 1891–2 and 1902–4, attracting huge crowds wherever it went; the first tours were seen by the queen and members of the royal family. Cody brought a genuine travelling history show of living exhibits from the western frontier of America. His troupe of over 800 included Annie Oakley, many native American 'Indians', cowboys and a menagerie including horses, buffalo, elks and longhorns. In June 1903 Buffalo Bill's Wild West Show was at the Pitchcroft, Worcester, where it seriously damaged the common pasture. During the 1902–4 tour 333 performances, including many on urban commons, were presented in different towns. Following Cody's success Wild West shows became popular in Britain and were copied for many years. Long-standing impersonators included Texas Bill Shufflebottom (Fig 7.5), 'English Buff Bill' and Ralf Norman 'the Silver Dollar King' (National Fairground Archive, University of Sheffield 2007b).

Figure 7.3
Jack Peaple's Revolving
Monoplanes, built in 1912,
in operation on Stafford
Common, presumably as
part of one of the travelling
fairs. The vehicle on which
the monoplanes were based
was a 'Growler', the taxi cab
of the day. The ride was so
well balanced that one push
set it spinning for hours.
[Reproduced courtesy of
Staffordshire Arts &
Museum Service]

Figure 7.4
Next to P T Barnum,
William F Cody (also known
as Buffalo Bill) was the
greatest showman of the
19th century. He pioneered
the Wild West Show as a
form of popular
entertainment on an
international scale.
[Denver Public Library,
Western History Collection,
Elliott & Fry, Z-2395]

Figure 7.5
The Shufflebottom family's
Wild West Show in 1936.
[Reproduced courtesy of the
National Fairground
Archive, University of
Sheffield Library]

Boxing

Boxing became popular in England during the late 17th century, as a mixture of knuckle fighting and wrestling. Boxing shows flourished at fairgrounds from the Restoration in 1660 onwards and in the early days the wealthy spectators would put up the prize money. During the 19th century and the first half of the 20th century boxing booths also formed part of travelling fairs. Prizefighting drew enthusiastic crowds to urban commons, where bare-knuckle contests, bouts with challengers from the crowd and professional matches were fought. One of the greatest fighters in the days of the bare-knuckle champions was Tom Hickman, who was known as the 'Gaslight Champion' because his punches caused the gaslights to go out. In 1821 he fought Bill Neat on Hungerford Downs in front of 25,000 spectators (National Fairground Archive, University of Sheffield 2007a). Tom Spring, later to become the All England Bare-Knuckle Champion, fought on Wimbledon Common in 1819. In 1824 Worcester was selected as the scene for Spring's fight with Irish champion John Langan. Although bare-knuckle fighting had been outlawed in 1750, local magistrates allowed the contest on the Pitchcroft to go ahead because a large contingent of influential aristocrats was expected to arrive. The fight drew around 50,000 people

to the town and makeshift stands were erected, two of which collapsed during the fight. Spring won the fight in the 77th round (Hurley 2002, 113–28). After the introduction of the Marquis of Queensberry rules in 1867, bare-knuckle fighting came to an end, but nevertheless the fairground boxing booth continued to be a cradle for the great British boxing hopes (Fig 7.6). During its history fighters such as Jem Mace, Kid Furness, Jimmy Wilde and Tommy Farr all fought in these booths. In their heyday each region of the country had three main booths travelling the fairground circuit with the boxers fighting for regional and national championships. Fairground boxing booths, with their brightly coloured frontages displaying the names and faces of boxing's heritage, are now a fading memory and have gone the way of other sideshows. This decline is linked to the decision by the Boxing Board of Control in 1947 to limit and partially restrict the use of boxers in the booths (National Fairground Archive, University of Sheffield 2007a).

Horse racing

Horse racing was, and still is, a popular activity on urban commons. While several racecourses on town commons are still in use, the remains of many more examples can be seen. Early horse races did not involve gambling and were

Figure 7.6
Hughes's boxers, 1916, at Heaton Park, Manchester. [Reproduced courtesy of the National Fairground Archive, University of Sheffield Library]

purely of local interest, though there were substantial prize stakes for the winners. The gentry gathered their coaches in the centre of the course and turned round to watch the progress of each race. Even in the most primitive period of the sport a stand, probably a wooden structure used by officials, and a permanent starting and winning post were present. The running track would be unenclosed, which made it necessary to 'make the way' whenever a race was held (Rice 1879, 27). The makeshift racing circuits found on urban commons had a tendency to be far from perfect. On Grimsby's East Marsh, two out of the three horses running for the Members' Plate fell into a sandpit and failed to finish in 1827 (Gillett 1970, 185). A 17th-century racecourse on Oxford's Port Meadow can be traced today through its causeways and bridges running across ditches and gravel workings (Lambrick and McDonald 1985, 100), while the track at Richmond, North Yorkshire, still survives as an earthwork with the ruin of its 19th-century grandstand.

During the 18th century some race meetings became splendid social occasions attracting the gentry and nobility (Fig 7.7). The meeting on Huntingdon's Portholme Meadow, for example, was described by Horace Walpole in 1760 as much more than a local affair and one of the nation's fashionable events of the year (*VCH Hunts II* 1932, 128–9). Perhaps the most prestigious and historic race meeting on an urban common, however, was the St Leger, held on Doncaster Town Moor, which began in 1778.

With the coming of the railways, race meetings changed in character as they became accessible to larger numbers of people. In 1860, 35 trains brought 50,000–60,000 people to Doncaster Town Moor on St Leger Day. Today the moor still provides the greater part of the racecourse's circuit, the level circular course of 1778 almost two miles long, with a National Hunt course inside it. An exercising course is slightly later, dating from 1793. On Newcastle Town Moor races were held from the early 18th century until 1882 and the remains of the course are among the most prominent earthworks on the moor. Archaeological survey in 1994 identified two phases to the circuit. They consisted of an early 1½-mile oval course visible as a 16.5m-wide terrace and a V-shaped ditch circumnavigating the high ground of Race Hill and changing to become two parallel ditches cutting through narrow ridge-and-furrow further down slope, and a later course following a similar line, but with a cutting and an embankment through Race Hill added to ease the gradient. The cutting is 150m long and

Figure 7.7
James Pollard's painting,
Doncaster Races, 1830–1:
Passing the Judges' Stand,
shows the racecourse on
Doncaster Town Moor.
[Virginia Museum of Fine Arts, Richmond. The Paul Mellon Collection. Photo: Katherine Wetzel.
© Virginia Museum of Fine Arts]

17m wide with the scarps of its stepped profile measuring up to 2.8m wide and 1.8m high. At its foot is a V-shaped drainage ditch 0.8m wide by 0.4m deep. A side ditch of the later course cuts the early course where the two merge. The finishing post and grandstand were situated to the north of Grandstand Road (Lofthouse 1995, 11–14).

Horse racing in Lincoln also has a long history involving different courses near the city. One course occupied West Common in the 1820s with as large a circuit as could be accommodated, which necessitated crossing a turnpike road twice. A later, shorter course ran alongside the realigned turnpike road. The fragmentary remains of this course can be seen describing a curvilinear arc defined by a bank and internal ditch on its outer side and by a bank alone on its inner side, all overlying ridge-and-furrow. The total width of the track is 18m. A slight ditch parallel to the course possibly marks the line of a spectator fence. The course continues northwards as a vegetation mark and southwards as a modern metalled track (Brown 2003, 7).

Other urban commons where horse racing took place included the Pitchcroft, Worcester, where an unusual 18th-century figure-of-eight course was superseded by the modern circuit. Races also took place from at least the 17th century on the common lands around York. In 1730 the York races were moved to the Knavesmire where permanent stands were erected in 1754 and 1965 (incorporating the surviving part of the 1754 stand). The August race meeting followed hangings at Tyburn. One notable race attracted 100,000 spectators to the common when, in 1804, Mrs Thornton, who rode side-saddle, challenged men to compete against her (Anon 1804a, 3; Anon 1804b, 3). Further racecourses once existed on, amongst others, Galleywood Common, Chelmsford; Clitheroe Town Moors; Marlborough Common; Tunbridge Wells Common; and Durdham Down, Bristol.

Despite its royal patronage and popular appeal, horse racing met with growing disapproval in some quarters for the vices associated with it. On Doncaster Town Moor, for example, gentlemen attending race meetings wore their swords and drank wine freely, so there were often disturbances. In 1615 an order was made to discontinue the races 'for the preventige of sutes, quarrels, murders, and bloodsheds that may ensue by the continuinge of the said race'

(Rice 1879, 26). In 1829 it took the combined forces of the Light Dragoons, West Yorkshire Militia, the Doncaster troop of the Yeomanry Cavalry, police officers and a body of mounted special constables including the mayor, the town clerk and Earl Fitzwilliam to disperse a lawless mob of 700 'thimble-riggers' armed with oak staves. In 1740 an Act of Parliament was passed stipulating that no plate of less value than £50 could be run for and imposing rules regarding weights and ownership of horses. In 1740 Parliament judged that horse racing had become too prevalent throughout the country for the welfare of 'idlers', who were supposed chiefly to attend race meetings (ibid, 15). Races on Tewkesbury's Severn Ham had distinguished patronage in 1721 and 1722, when the Prince of Wales (later George II) gave gold cups as racing prizes, but during the 19th century they were discontinued because some town inhabitants objected to the 'loose characters' they attracted (Pain 1992, 7). By the mid-19th century there was also concern about the character of the races on Stafford Common. After attempts to put the meeting on 'a firm and respectable foundation' by ensuring the 'patronage and attendance of neighbouring gentry' proved futile, the races were discontinued (VCH Staffs II 1967, 366–7); however, by the early part of the 20th century they had resumed on Whit Mondays as an ad hoc affair. Jumps were made from hurdles and gorse by the Common Keeper and horses taking part were owned by local people. These races continued until 1936. There were also motorcycle races, dog races and running races (Mrs M Bolton, pers comm).

Religious gatherings and political rallies

Urban commons provided large open spaces in towns where crowds of people were able to congregate freely and religious meetings or spontaneous political gatherings frequently took place on them. An early example was on Clitheroe Moor where a meeting took place as part of the 1536 Pilgrimage of Grace in opposition to the religious changes made by Henry VIII (VCH Lancs VI 1911, 349). In later centuries large crowds gathered on urban commons to hear renowned preachers. For instance 30,000 people flocked to hear George Whitefield (pronounced Whitfield) when he addressed crowds from the ancient long barrow

on Minchinhampton Common in 1739 and it thereafter became known as 'Whitfield's Tump' (*see* Fig 2.1). Both Whitefield and John Wesley made regular appearances on other urban commons (Fig 7.8).

Kennington Common, London, was described as, 'a favourite spot for merryandrews and other buffooneries in open rivalry and competition with field preachers and ranters. It was here that Mr Maw-worm encountered the brickbats of his congregation and had his "pious tail" illuminated with the squibs and crackers of the unregenerate' (Walford 1878, 338). In his journal entry for 6 May 1739, Whitefield wrote:

At six preached at Kennington. Such a sight I never saw before. I believe there were no less than fifty thousand people, and near fourscore coaches, besides great numbers of horses. There was such an awful silence amongst them. God gave me great enlargement of heart. I continued my discourse for an hour and a half and when I returned home I was filled with such love, peace and joy that I cannot express it.

(Whitefield 1965, 262)

In the same year Charles Wesley recorded in his diary entry for 24 June that he 'walked onto the [Kennington] Common and cried to multitudes upon multitudes, "Repent ye, and believe in the Gospel"' (Wesley 1909, 241).

Urban commons also have a long history as places of popular dissent. At Weybridge in 1649 a group of local people – later to become known as 'The Diggers' – gathered on St George's Hill, Weybridge Heath, and began to dig to represent a symbolic assumption of the ownership of the common lands. Digger colonies began to appear on common lands elsewhere, but the community ended in 1650 when their leader, Gerrard Winstanley, and others were indicted for disorderly and unlawful assembly (Hill 1991).

The late 19th century was a period of social upheaval and instability, which was reflected in the nature of gatherings on urban commons. The progress of enclosure, culminating in the General Enclosure Acts in the 19th century, created large private landed estates; this, combined with new mechanisation in agriculture, caused many landless labourers and small farmers to leave the countryside for work in expanding industrial towns. There, popular discontent bred in the overcrowded slums that sprung up close to factories. Brandon Hill, Bristol's oldest open public space, became notorious as a venue for riotous public meetings at this time. Rights of unrestricted association on the hill and contention over civic polity were seen throughout the 18th century. In 1716 and 1718, in open defiance of the Whig Corporation, Jacobites used it for anti-Hanoverian revels and in 1745 a confederacy of over 1,000 striking sailors gathered to pass resolutions demanding higher pay. The authorities, recognising the significance of the hill, used it for displays of official power such as the execution of deserter John Faulkner, who was shot on the summit in 1771 before a large crowd. In the aftermath of the French Revolution, when oppositional meetings were excluded from public buildings, Brandon Hill was also used for electioneering and there were mass meetings there following Manchester's Peterloo Massacre of 1819. The most notable event took place in 1832, after the enfranchisement of a small section of the middle classes by the passing of the Great Reform Act. A celebratory banquet organised by the beneficiaries roused popular discontent in the city and barricades around the hill were overwhelmed by a multitude of 14,000 people who ate the food, drank the beer, danced on the tables, robbed people of hats and shoes, and rolled barrels of beer down the hill to the poorer districts of the city (Fig 7.9). During the 1830s Brandon Hill became a meeting place for the

Figure 7.8
George Whitefield was a popular field preacher of the mid-18th century, often appearing on urban commons. He wrote: 'I thought it might be doing the service of my creator, who had a mountain for a pulpit, and the heavens for a sounding board; and who … sent his servants into the highways and hedges' (Gillies 1837, 38).

National Union of the Working Classes and the Chartists tried to hold mass meetings there. In 1842 proposed meetings during the general strike were dispersed by police and magistrates. The wealthy citizens of Clifton eventually created gardens on the top of the hill to inhibit its use for meetings and the Cabot Tower was constructed, commemorating the mercantile explorer John Cabot (Poole 1999, 51–3).

Kennington Common (now Kennington Park), in Lambeth, was also the scene of popular protests. The Great Chartist Meeting, held there in 1848, awoke fear of insurrection and prompted unparalleled military preparations by the government (Fig 7.10). The common was turned into a park in order to put an end to uncontrolled public assembly, so suffering a similar fate to Brandon Hill. The racecourse on Epsom Downs was a further scene for protest and became renowned as the site of the martyrdom of Emily Davison in the cause of female suffrage in 1913.

Fairs and celebrations

Throughout history urban commons have been the place where town celebrations have taken place. These include the Leicester Freemen's Common Festival, described in 1849 as 'debasing in immorality, excess in drunkenness and obscenity in levity' (Elliott 2000, 167). Other events were open to all, such as the Hoppings Fair on Newcastle Town Moor (*see* Fig 8.5), its name probably deriving from the 'hopping' or dancing that occurred there (Newcastle City Council 2004) or from the Anglo-Saxon word 'hoppen', meaning fair (The Freemen of the City of Newcastle upon Tyne 2008). This fair accompanied the race meetings on the Town Moor during the 18th century. When the races were moved from the Town Moor in 1882, a temperance festival grew up in its place (Lofthouse 1995, 19). In Cambridge an annual fair

on Midsummer Common originated in rights held by Barnwell Priory, which were sold to the corporation in 1505. Royal jubilees, coronations and the ending of wars were also celebrated on most urban commons. On the Pitchcroft, Worcester, jubilee celebrations in 1887 and 1935, peace celebrations in 1902 and 1918, and Empire Day celebrations in 1917 were among such events.

Civil aviation

For pioneers in aviation urban commons provided what was often the only suitable land close to towns for use as take-off and landing sites. For instance 'The Quarry' in Shrewsbury hosted hot-air balloons in 1898. From their earliest days aeroplanes also landed and took off from urban commons to the amazement of townsfolk. The construction and testing of Blériot-type aeroplanes took place at Portholme Aerodrome, Huntingdon, in the early 1900s. In 1910, when James Radley made the first flight from the common, virtually the whole of Godmanchester and Huntingdon turned out to watch. Crowds later flocked to see other early aviators trying out their flying machines (Huntingdonshire Local Hist Soc 1992).

Flying soon developed into a spectator sport and urban commons were often the sites for

aviation displays in the early 20th century. One such display – the Doncaster Aviation Meeting, billed as 'the first ever flying meeting in England' – took place on Doncaster Town Moor in October 1909 (Fig 7.11). It was attended by tens of thousands of people and the competitors included Colonel Samuel Cody in a biplane, four pilots in Blériot monoplanes, one in a 'dirigible balloon', an all-British biplane said to be the smallest in the world and a Wright biplane (the first of its kind on wheels). The flying area in the centre of the common formed a circuit of 1½ miles, the turning points being marked by tall posts known as pylons. On the Pitchcroft, Worcester, there were aircraft displays before and after the First World War, and W Gooden, an early aviator, was a visitor there (Jones 1998, 30–1).

As the 20th century progressed, urban commons began to host commercial flights. They operated from the Pitchcroft, Worcester, between 1919 and 1927, while a biplane flying from London Airport by Imperial Airways landed on the Knavesmire, York, during the 1920s. During the 1930s pleasure trips could be made from the Pitchcroft in an aircraft operated by Sir Alan Cobham and his 'Flying Circus' (ibid, 33). As commercial flights increased in number, airports were constructed and the roughness of the terrain of urban commons and their proximity to housing meant that they could no longer provide suitable airstrips for larger, faster and increasingly sophisticated aircraft.

Today's events

Today town populations with far more leisure time than their forebears have increased recreational pressure on urban commons. Their use for spontaneous games continues and fairs and circuses are still frequent events (*see* Fig 8.4). Bare-knuckle boxing, freak shows and other vestiges of the past have long since disappeared, but new events have replaced them in the town calendar. For example many urban commons host events such as car boot sales throughout the year. Classic car rallies attract enthusiasts to Harpenden and Southsea Commons. Streatham Common, London, has a kite day, while Clapham Common hosts the annual Urban Games (*see* Fig 8.3). A rock concert, 'Power in the Park', is a new event held each summer on Southampton Common.

Figure 7.11
The aviation meeting of October 1909 on Doncaster Town Moor was claimed to be the first of its kind in Britain and drew large crowds.
[Donny Online, www.donny.co.uk]

8

Present and future

The value of town commons

Port Meadow and Wolvercote Common in Oxford are now unique in their region in terms of their ecology because of the destruction of hay meadows since 1945. Their common status has protected them from ploughing, draining and the application of chemical fertiliser, allowing the continued evolution of grassland communities developed through traditional management by farmers exercising ancient rights of intercommoning. This ecological significance led to designation of these and adjacent smaller commons as Sites of Special Scientific Interest (SSSIs) in 1952 (55 per cent of all commons are SSSIs). The combination of ecological and archaeological significance of Port Meadow, combined with its historical associations and value as an amenity for the people of Oxford, is outstanding. And yet, as is the case with other urban commons, it is consistently undervalued in terms of designation and under-managed by the responsible authorities (Lambrick and McDonald 1985), perhaps because it is taken for granted.

Urban commons today provide semi-natural habitats for wildlife and a delicate balance exists between farming, leisure interests and nature conservation. The decline in grazing has caused colonisation of some urban commons by scrub which can be detrimental to their biodiversity. Mousehold Heath, Norwich, has suffered from a lack of grazing, causing the majority of its area to change from open heath to woodland within the last hundred years.

In Bristol the cessation of grazing also had a profound effect on the downs landscape (Goldthorpe 2006, 28). Traditional farming regimes maintained on other urban commons provide rich havens for wildlife. Portholme Meadow, Huntingdon, managed as a traditional Lammas meadow, is an SSSI and a Special Area of Conservation. Big Meadow, Loughborough, another SSSI, is now a nature reserve owned by the Leicestershire and Rutland Wildlife Trust. It is subject to common rights and has been managed as a flood meadow for as long as records exist. Because so many town commons are on valley floors they are prone to flooding (Fig 8.1). The incidence of such flooding will vary naturally with climate change but panic measures to prevent or control flooding may be damaging in themselves; for example Port Meadow, Oxford, is under new threat from proposed flood alleviation schemes (McDonald 2007, ix). At the same time it is anticipated that 'historic open spaces in urban areas will play an important role in ameliorating the effects of a hotter climate' (English Heritage 2008, 12). Biodiversity Action Plans are now in place for several areas, which include town commons such as Staines Moor, and there are numerous local authority countryside management projects tackling habitat restoration.

The uses to which the surviving urban commons are put are many and varied. Not all are universally approved: '…if it had not been for the stubborn defence by Newbury commoners of their rights to Greenham Common, where on earth could NATO have parked its nukes?' asked E P Thompson, with tongue firmly in cheek (1991, 126). Thompson reminds us that Greenham Common (Fig 8.2) has a history of controversy: "A regularly organised mob of many hundreds of the most abandoned and dissolute characters" threw down an encloser's fences "with most terrific hooting and abuse"… in 1842' (ibid, n3).

More popular uses of urban commons include their continued attraction as venues for fairs, festivals, sporting events and circuses (Figs 8.3 and 8.4), from the Hoppings Fair on Newcastle Town Moor (Fig 8.5) to the Cavaliers' Week Fire on Great Torrington Common (*see* Fig 6.1) – though increased insurance costs

Figure 8.1
Tewkesbury in flood,
November 2000: the Severn
Ham is under water beyond
the abbey in the left
foreground.
[NMR 18830/07]

Figure 8.2
Greenham Common,
Newbury.
[NMR 21864/12]

Figure 8.3 (above, left) Urban Games, Clapham Common, 22 July 2005. [NMR DP000897]

Figure 8.4 (above, right) Troupe Tamerlan performing at Gifford's Circus. [Andrew Rees, © andrewreesphotography. co.uk]

and tighter health-and-safety measures have sometimes threatened such events.

Recent research into the governance and management of commons has followed the development of the idea of the 'stakeholder' (eg Short and Winter 1999). This research and the guidance built on it (eg Short *et al* 2005) has, naturally, tended to concentrate on the rural scene but has lessons for urban commons. It has also stressed the importance of the historical aspects of commons: '... only by understanding the development of commons, particularly in their legislative history, can we hope to make sense of the complexities they present in terms of governance' (Short and Winter 1999, 614–15). There is less appreciation of the archaeological aspects – the physical remains of past activities – though it is certainly not ignored and there has been a recent upsurge in interest. This has led, for instance, to a rapid assessment of London's commons for English Heritage (Lambert and Williams 2005) and the inclusion of archaeological interests in *Common Vision*, a DVD presentation produced by Hampshire County Council in 2008 on the management of commons for local communities.

The legal situation has now been changed by the passing of the Commons Act 2006. This act repeals the Commons Act of 1285, which – with additional acts in 1876, 1893 and 1899, for instance – had formed the basis for the protection and regulation of common land. The new Commons Act 2006 enables more sustainable management of commons through 'commons councils', bringing together commoners and landowners to regulate grazing and other activities, and reinforcing existing protections against abuse, encroachment and unauthorised development. This should bring more common land that has been neglected into 'good' or 'recovering' condition. The act stresses the natural diversity of commons and their value as wildlife habitats, with much less emphasis on their historical and archaeological value; nevertheless, the historic environment should benefit. It also sets new clear criteria for the registration of town and village greens, giving them permanent protection. It also allows for the registration of previously 'missed' commons.

The English Heritage project

Genesis of the project

The reasons for undertaking the project have been briefly described in Chapter 1 – urban commons are under pressure and because their historic element is not understood they are unprotected. At the outset of the project it was noted that:

Urban commons are an almost unexplored archaeological resource; indeed, their survival has not been reviewed on any national or regional basis. Nevertheless, they offer the opportunity to extend our attention within the historic urban agenda to a wider range of archaeological phenomena, and to a broader topography beyond the built-up core that has generally been the focus of study. These commons can also offer a new window of understanding into the development of the adjacent town or city. This is a matter of recognising what has previously been 'not known because not looked for'.

Just as importantly, such open spaces are critically important in the modern urban fabric. For the inhabitants of a town they are key components in what they

would understand as their 'historic environment' as it impacts on their daily lives. They are almost chronically under pressure, both from major developments and from more insidious and cumulative causes. They, typically, have no Conservation Plan. Their detailed historic environment content and its value are certainly unknown and therefore deliver no conservation benefits.

EH has current initiatives within its urban research framework addressed at urban parks and cemeteries. This Proposal directs attention to another sort of urban space. It seeks to establish ways of placing Historic Environment value on locations that are undoubtedly publicly valued. It also seeks to highlight, by example, the recognition and use of those HE values, both by local authorities and the public.

(Everson and Bowden 2002)

The aim of the project was therefore, as stated above, to investigate the archaeological content and Historic Environment value of urban commons in England and to prompt appropriate conservation strategies for them. The legal situation has changed since the inception of the project because of the Commons Act 2006.

Figure 8.5
The Hoppings Fair on Newcastle Town Moor in 1964.
[Reproduced courtesy of the National Fairground Archive, University of Sheffield Library]

Project methodology

The objectives of the project were to research and survey a representative sample of urban commons in England (*see* Fig 1.2); to make available the results of that work in the most appropriate ways to the widest constituency (this book, highlighting both historical and conservation aspects, is a prime part of that objective); and, through partnership arrangements where possible, to promote and underpin local community conservation initiatives.

The first task was therefore a desktop exercise to identify possible surviving urban commons. This was undertaken through a literature search, much assisted by the existence of the results of a parliamentary enquiry into urban commons in 1870. This resulted in a 'Primary List', which has now grown to nearly 320 English towns possessing commons at some time in the past (*see* Gazetteer). This list identified those where some physical survival of the commons was known or might be expected. Forms of survival might include preservation of earthworks but could also include areas of open space landscaped for

parks or playing fields where survival of archaeological features might only be recoverable through aerial photography or other means. At the other end of the scale, 'survival' might only be through the distinctiveness of the street pattern in housing estates built over former commons.

Given the difficulty in defining urban commons (*see* Chapter 1), it was decided that any common attached to a settlement that had at one time become or been a town, such as Godalming or Minchinhampton, would be a candidate for detailed study but that towns built over and extinguishing commons, such as Brighton, were not. Fieldwork would necessarily have to be restricted to a small sample of the 25 or more towns where some level of survival was initially identified by this exercise. It was decided to seek to include a range of sizes of towns, small as well as large; to consider cases where commons have been built over and lost, and investigate the processes and distinctive results of this; to ensure, as far as possible, a national spread of examples; and to be aware of and draw on substantial and relevant work already undertaken by others (for example, on

Port Meadow at Oxford). The location of field-work, however, is governed by practicalities and there is some inevitable unevenness in geographical coverage (*see* Fig 1.2). London's commons, for instance, did not figure largely in the project fieldwork though they are clearly more prominent in the literature than are the commons of other towns.

It was agreed at the outset that in a few cases, where earthwork survival was particularly good and appeared to be especially informative, a comprehensive and detailed large-scale (Level 3) survey should be carried out (English Heritage 2007a; Fig 8.6); however, in most cases it was decided that survey should be selective and at Levels 2 or 1 (less detailed and typically carried out at smaller scales). Some existing completed Level 3 work (as at Newcastle upon Tyne and Minchinhampton) would clearly be directly relevant to the project as would the then ongoing work by English Heritage's Archaeological Survey and Investigation team for outside partners, such as the survey of Corfe Common undertaken for the National Trust (Fletcher 2003). An Oxford MSt dissertation – undertaken in 2002–3 and supervised by Mark Bowden, one of the authors – presented a study of urban commons in Oxfordshire (Connor 2003). Fresh field survey and investigation directly for the project was carried out between 2003 and 2005. Five commons were surveyed at Level 3, 2 at Level 2 and 50 at Level 1. The Level 3 surveys took full advantage of relatively new technological developments in Differential Global Positioning by Satellite (GPS) survey (English Heritage 2003). However, in many cases the complexity of the earthworks, or dense tree cover, made the employment of more traditional techniques necessary (English Heritage 2002). One Level 2 survey, on Stafford Common, was the opportunity for trialling a new survey technique employing the latest generation of more accurate hand-held GPS receivers, while the common and Freeman's Marsh at Hungerford were surveyed by transcription of aerial photographs (Newsome 2005).

This book is one outcome of the project, aiming to present the most significant results and celebrating these special areas, but it is by no means a definitive statement. Archaeological research should, and no doubt will, continue and new discoveries will be made and new questions and ideas formulated. This project was intended to promote the view that

landscape archaeology is about the fabric of the land as created and modified over a long period and in which our own activities are part of that continuum. This reflects the changing nature of archaeology as a discipline that is increasingly concerned with public understanding, along with land management and conservation.

Future conservation work on town commons

This project has looked at a sample of urban commons and does not pretend to present a total picture of the surviving archaeological remains in these places. Nor has our survey been by any means exhaustive. At Biggleswade, for instance, we have merely noted the existence of a potentially very significant surviving segment of prehistoric, Romano-British and medieval landscape (Fig 8.7); large-scale survey

Figure 8.7
Possible Roman villa or temple complex at the northern end of Biggleswade Common (looking south), showing up well in dry conditions in July 1990. In most aerial photographs the cropmarks in the cultivated strip (foreground) show better than the surviving earthworks (beyond the drainage cut). This phenomenon occurs all around the common and has led to the under-recording of the surviving earthworks on the common itself. [NMR 4385/19A]

work is required here to analyse and understand the detail of this remarkable multi-layered survival. Though rare, this is unlikely to be a unique instance.

But any further archaeological work – be it undertaken by national agencies, local units, academic institutions or, perhaps more properly, by local independent archaeologists – should only be a precursor to more work on the sympathetic management and conservation of these now-rare survivals. Sympathetic management will depend on measured responses to climate change, especially in respect of flooding and global warming (English Heritage 2008) but also to the particular activities that tend to take place on town commons, such as golf (English Heritage 2007b). Information, training and guidance on such matters are available through HELM (Historic Environment Local Management – www.helm.org.uk). However, the recognition of town commons as a valid historical entity and a valued part of the modern urban environment, which this English Heritage project has sought to establish, is an essential first step towards successful informed conservation.

An overridingly important consideration for the future is maintaining the character of urban (and indeed all) commons as clearly different from parks and public gardens. The fact that they are no longer, generally, working as agricultural commons should not mean that they are treated as urban parks. Where there is still traditional grazing on town commons, the local interest is strong; those who graze their horses on Lincoln's West Common, for instance, are very much involved in the management of the common. Elsewhere local involvement is more muted. The common overseers and their assistants mentioned in Chapter 3 were presumably drawn from the local community; management of the commons now is largely in the hands of local authorities and arranged by statutory bodies, such as Natural England. The Commons Act 2006 has introduced the possibility of forming commons councils so that local people can again manage and enjoy these places as active participants, developing their interest in both their natural and historical aspects. While the idea of commons councils is aimed primarily at rural, and especially upland, commons, town commons might also benefit from this 'bottom-up' approach that brings all the stakeholders together.

GAZETTEER

The gazetteer has been compiled from the 1870 Parliamentary Return of all towns which had at that time, or were known to have had in the past, common lands, and from numerous other sources. The omission of a town or city from this gazetteer does not imply that it has not, or never had, common lands – only that no evidence has been noted in the course of the English Heritage project. The present, not historical, county or local authority is listed.

Places marked with asterisks are those where some degree of physical survival of the common lands has been noted in the course of the English Heritage project. One asterisk indicates slight survival, in the form of the current street pattern for instance. Four asterisks represent considerable extant commons with good survival of features of archaeological and historical interest. However, it should be noted that this ranking is based upon subjective judgement and sometimes limited evidence.

Town name	Town commons mentioned by name in the text	County/LA	Survival?
Abingdon	Abingdon Common	Oxon	*
Accrington		Lancs	*
Aldeburgh		Suff	
Aldershot		Hants	
Alnmouth	Alnmouth Common	Northum	
Alnwick		Northum	
Alston		Cumb	**
Altrincham		Trafford	
Amersham		Bucks	
Amesbury		Wilts	
Andover		Hants	
Appleby		Cumb	*
Arundel		W Suss	
Ashby-de-la-Zouche		Leics	
Atherstone		Warks	
Axbridge		Som	
Axminster		Devon	
Aylesbury		Bucks	
Bakewell		Derbys	
Bampton		Oxon	**
Banbury		Oxon	*
Barnard Castle		Co Durham	
Basingstoke		Hants	
Bath		BaNES	
Batley		Yorks	

Town name	Town commons mentioned by name in the text	County/LA	Survival?
Beaminster	Beaminster Down	Dorset	
Beccles		Suff	
Bedford		Beds	
Berkhamsted	Berkhamsted Common	Herts	
Berwick		Northum	
Beverley	Figham Common; Hurn Common; Swine Moor; Westwood Common	E Yorks	****
Biggleswade	Biggleswade Common	Beds	****
Birmingham		Birmingham	
Bishop's Castle		Salop	
Bishop's Stortford		Herts	
Bodmin		Cornw	*
Bolton		Lancs	
Boroughbridge		N Yorks	
Boscastle		Cornw	*
Bossiney		Cornw	
Bournemouth		Dorset	
Bradford	Baildon Bank and Moor	Bradford Dist	
Brading (IoW)		Hants	
Bradninch		Devon	
Brampton		Cumb	
Brandon		Suff	***
Bridlington		E Yorks	
Brighton		Brighton & Hove	
Bristol	Brandon Hill; Clifton Down; Durdham Down	Bristol	**
Brixham		Devon	*
Bromley		Greater London	
Bromsgrove		Worcs	
Brough		Cumb	
Burford	High Mead	Oxon	**
Burton-upon-Trent		Staffs	
Bury St Edmund		Suff	
Calne		Wilts	
Cambridge	Donkey's Common; Laundress Green; Midsummer Common; Port Field (later Carme Field); Scholars' Piece	Cambs	**
Carlisle		Cumb	
Chatteris		Cambs	
Chelmsford	Galleywood Common	Essex	
Cheltenham		Glos	
Chesham		Bucks	
Chester	The Roodee	Ches	*
Chester-le-Street		Co Durham	
Chichester	Portfield	W Suss	
Chippenham	West Mead	Wilts	

Town name	Town commons mentioned by name in the text	County/LA	Survival?
Chipping Norton		Oxon	***
Chorley		Lancs	*
Christchurch		Dorset	*
Cirencester		Glos	
Clitheroe	Clitheroe Town Moors	Lancs	*
Coalville		Leics	
Cobham		Surrey	
Cockermouth		Cumb	
Colchester		Essex	*
Congleton		Ches	
Corfe	Corfe Common	Dorset	****
Coventry		Warks	
Cricklade	Cricklade Common	Wilts	***
Croston		Lancs	
Croydon		Greater London	
Dalton		Cumb	
Darlington		Co Durham	
Dartford		Kent	*
Daventry		Northants	
Deddington		Oxon	
Derby		Derbys	
Dewsbury		Kirklees Dist	
Diss		Norf	*
Doncaster	Doncaster Town Moor	Doncaster Dist	***
Dorking	Cotmandene Chart	Surrey	
Dudley		Dudley	
Dunwich		Suff	
Durham		Co Durham	
East Dereham		Norf	
East Retford		Notts	
Egremont		Cumb	
Ely		Cambs	**
Epsom & Walton	Epsom Downs	Surrey	*
Erith		Greater London	
Esher	Ditton Common	Surrey	
Evesham		Worcs	
Exeter		Devon	*
Eye		Suff	
Fakenham		Norf	
Fareham		Hants	
Farnborough		Hants	
Farnham		Surrey	
Flookburgh		Cumb	
Folkestone		Kent	

GAZETTEER

Town name	Town commons mentioned by name in the text	County/LA	Survival?
Fordwich		Kent	
Gainsborough		Lincs	
Gateshead		Gateshead	
Glastonbury	Common Moor	Som	
Glossop		Derbys	
Gloucester		Glos	
Godalming		Surrey	**
Godmanchester		Cambs	
Grantham		Lincs	
Great Malvern	Malvern Common	Worcs	
Great Torrington	Great Torrington Common	Devon	**
Greystoke		Cumb	*
Grimsby	East Marsh; West Marsh	Lincs	
Guildford		Surrey	
Hadleigh		Suff	
Halesowen		Dudley	
Halifax		Calderdale Dist	
Harpenden	Harpenden Common	Herts	
Harrogate	Harrogate Stray	N Yorks	**
Hartlepool		Cleve	
Haverhill		Suff	
Hedon		E Yorks	*
Hemel Hempstead		Herts	
Hereford		Herefs	*
Hertford	Hartham Common; King's Meads	Herts	**
High Wycombe		Bucks	
Higham Ferrers		Northants	
Hinckley		Leics	*
Hitchin		Herts	
Hornby		Lancs	
Hornsea		E Yorks	
Huddersfield		Kirklees Dist	
Hungerford	Freeman's Marsh; Hungerford Common (originally Port Down Common)	Berks	****
Huntingdon	Portholme Meadow; Walnut Tree Common	Cambs	**
Ilkley	Ilkley Moor	Bradford Dist	**
Ipswich		Suff	
Kendal	Kendal Fell	Cumb	**
Keswick		Cumb	
Kettering		Northants	
Kidderminster		Worcs	
King's Lynn		Norf	
Kirkby Lonsdale		Cumb	
Kirkby Stephen		Cumb	

Town name	Town commons mentioned by name in the text	County/LA	Survival?
Kirkham		Lancs	
Knaresborough		N Yorks	
Lancaster		Lancs	
Launceston		Cornw	
Ledbury		Herefs	
Leeds		Leeds Dist	
Leek		Staffs	
Leicester		Leics	*
Leighton Buzzard		Beds	
Leominster		Herefs	
Lewes		E Suss	
Lichfield		Staffs	
Lincoln	Cow Paddle; Monk's Leys Common; South Common; West Common	Lincs	****
Liskeard		Cornw	
Liverpool		Liverpool	
London	Blackheath Common; Chelsea Common; Clapham Common; Eltham Common; Hammersmith Common; Hampstead Heath; Kennington Common; Moorfields; Streatham Common; Wandsworth Common	Greater London	
Looe		Cornw	*
Loughborough	Big Meadow	Leics	**
Lowestoft		Suff	
Ludlow		Salop	*
Luton		Beds	*
Lutterworth		Leics	
Lydd	East Ripe; West Ripe	Kent	**
Macclesfield		Ches	
Maidenhead		Berks	*
Maidstone		Kent	
Malmesbury	Portmannesheath	Wilts	
Maltby		Rotherham	
Malton		N Yorks	
Manchester	Heaton Park; Kersal Moor; Wardle Common	Manchester	
March		Cambs	
Market Rasen		Lincs	
Marlborough	Marlborough Common; Marlborough Downs; Portfield	Wilts	**
Masham		N Yorks	
Matlock		Derbys	
Melton Mowbray		Leics	
Minchinhampton	Minchinhampton Common	Glos	****
Morpeth		Northum	*
Nantwich		Ches	*
Newark		Notts	
Newbury	Crookham Common; Greenham Common	Berks	

Town name	Town commons mentioned by name in the text	County/LA	Survival?
Newcastle under Lyme		Staffs	
Newcastle upon Tyne	Castle Leazes; Duke's Moor; Hunter's Moor; Little Moor; Newcastle Town Moor; Nuns Moor	Newcastle	****
Newmarket		Suff	
Newport (IoW)		Hants	
Newport Pagnell		Bucks	
Newquay		Cornw	
Northallerton		N Yorks	
Northampton	Cow Meadow	Northants	*
Norwich	Chapel Fields; Mousehold Heath	Norf	*
Nottingham		Notts	*
Nuneaton		Warks	
Okehampton	Okehampton Common	Devon	*
Oldham		Oldham	
Ormskirk	Ormskirk Moss	Lancs	
Oswestry		Salop	
Oundle		Northants	
Oxford	Port Meadow; Wolvercote Common	Oxon	***
Padstow		Cornw	
Paignton		Devon	
Penrith		Cumb	
Penwortham		Lancs	
Pershore		Worcs	
Peterborough	Borough Fen	Cambs	
Petersfield	Petersfield Heath Common	Hants	***
Pevensey		E Suss	
Pickering		N Yorks	
Plumstead		Greater London	
Plympton		Devon	
Pontefract		Wakefield Dist	
Poole	Canford Heath	Dorset	**
Portsea		Hants	
Prescot		Knowsley	
Preston	Moor Park	Lancs	*
Queenborough		Kent	
Reading		Berks	
Reigate	Banstead Heath; Earlswood Common	Surrey	
Richmond		N Yorks	**
Ripon		N Yorks	
Rochdale		Rochdale Dist	
Rotherham		Rotherham Dist	
Rugby		Warks	
Rugeley		Staffs	

Town name	Town commons mentioned by name in the text	County/LA	Survival?
Ruyton		Salop	
Rye		E Suss	
Saffron Walden		Suff	***
Sandbach		Ches	
Scarborough		N Yorks	
Sedbergh		Cumb	
Settle		Yorks	
Shaftesbury		Dorset	
Sheffield	Assembly Green, Brightside; Crooks Moor	Sheffield Dist	
Shrewsbury	'The Quarry'	Salop	**
Sleaford		Lincs	
Skipton		N Yorks	
Southampton	Southampton Common	Hants	**
Southsea	Southsea Common	Hants	
Southwold		Suff	
Sowerby		Calderdale Dist	
St Ives		Cambs	
St Ives		Cornw	
St Neots		Cambs	
Stafford	Stafford Common	Staffs	***
Staines	Staines Moor	Surrey	**
Stamford		Lincs	**
Stockbridge		Hants	
Stockport		Stockport	
Stone		Staffs	
Stratford-upon-Avon		Warks	
Sudbury	King's Marsh; North Meadow Common	Suff	***
Sunderland		Sunderland	
Sutton Coldfield	Sutton Park	Birmingham	***
Swaffham		Norf	
Tadcaster		N Yorks	
Tamworth		Warks	
Tavistock		Devon	
Tetbury		Glos	
Tewkesbury	Severn Ham	Glos	**
Thame		Oxon	
Thaxted		Essex	
Thetford		Norf	
Thirsk		N Yorks	
Towcester		Northants	
Tregony		Cornw	
Tring		Herts	
Tunbridge Wells	Rusthall Common; Tunbridge Wells Common	Kent	**

Town name	Town commons mentioned by name in the text	County/LA	Survival?
Ulverston		Cumb	**
Uppingham		Leics	
Upton-on-Severn		Worcs	
Wakefield	Holme Moor (or Common Heath)	Wakefield Dist	
Wallingford		Oxon	**
Walsall		Walsall	
Wantage		Oxon	
Ware		Herts	
Wareham		Dorset	**
Warminster		Wilts	**
Warwick		Warks	
Watford		Herts	
Wells		Som	
Wendover		Bucks	
West Bromwich		Sandwell	
Weybridge	Weybridge Heath	Surrey	
Weymouth		Dorset	
Whitby		N Yorks	
Whitehaven		Cumb	
Whitstable		Kent	
Whitworth	Whitworth and Trough Common	Lancs	*
Wigan		Lancs	*
Wigton		Cumb	
Wilmslow		Ches	
Wilton		Wilts	
Wimbledon	Wimbledon Common	Greater London	**
Wimborne		Dorset	
Wisbech		Cambs	
Woking	Horsell Common; St John's Lye	Surrey	
Wolverhampton		Wolverhampton	
Woodstock		Oxon	
Woolwich	Woolwich Common	Greater London	
Worcester	Moorsfields; Pitchcroft	Worcs	**
Workington		Cumb	
Worksop		Notts	
Wymondham		Norf	
York	Bootham Stray; Hob Moor; Knavesmire; Micklegate Stray; Walmgate Stray	N Yorks	****

REFERENCES

Primary sources

Bristol Record Office: 34901/206 Agreement between G W Daubeney and commoners regarding laying drains across part of Durdham Down, 1897

Gloucestershire County Record Office: A17/3 Way leave agreements for telegraph poles, overhead electricity cables and main pipes on the Severn Ham, Tewkesbury

Lincoln Reference Library: Abell Collection, *Agriculture & Commons* **1**

Lincolnshire Archives:

Hill 12 Records of the First Lincolnshire Rifle Volunteer Corps, 1859–97

L1/1/9 Minutes of the proceedings of the Mayor, Aldermen and Citizens of the City of Lincoln

L1/1/20/1 Lincoln City: Proceedings of Commons and Markets Committee, 1883–87

L1/1/20/9 Lincoln City: Proceedings of Commons and Markets Committee, 1913–23

Minutes of Arboretum Committee 20 Nov 1883–24 Feb 1890

Sibthorp Scrapbook

London Metropolitan Archives: ACC/1016/485 Notice issued to the commoners of Tottenham by the East London Waterworks Company, 1868 (part of a collection of papers from Couchmans, Surveyors and Valuers, Tottenham, Middlesex)

NMR: NMR numbers (eg NMR: SU 72 SE 18) are given for sites for which there is no readily available published reference; these numbers consist of the OS 1:10,000 quarter-sheet reference plus a unique number, from which details can be obtained through the NMR AMIE database.

Nottinghamshire Archives: DD/2402/1/3 The letters of Thomas Moore Emmanual to his parents 1916–1918

Parliamentary Return 1870: *Return of all Boroughs and Cities in the United Kingdom possessing Common or other Lands, in respect of which the Freemen or other privileged Inhabitants claim any exclusive Right of Property or Use, and distinguishing those Places in which such privileged Inhabitants claim any Parliamentary or Municipal Franchise, or any Immunity from Tolls or Dues paid by other Inhabitants*

Society of Antiquaries of Newcastle upon Tyne Collection: PM32, T Oliver 1852 Plan of the ancient boundary of the Town and County of Newcastle upon Tyne, also of the Town Moor and Castle Leazes, showing the drains and the intakes

Staffordshire Record Office: D1323/H/3, *Minute Book of Stafford Commoners*, 1820

TNA:

AIR 1/679/21/13/2203 Establishment of Aircraft Acceptance Parks

WO 32/5946 Training: General (Code 35A): Acquisition of common land in Kington and Putney for military training. Memorandum on the use of common land for military training by Treasury Solicitor, 1876

WO 32/9060 Experiments at Lydd: Report of Ordnance Committee

WO 32/18451 Plumstead Common, London: Right of War Department to use common for training

WO 78/2890 Woolwich Common

York City Archives: F7/205, *Minutes of Court of Quarter Sessions of the Peace*, 1647–9

Secondary sources

Aitchison, J, Crowther, K, Ashby, M and Redgrave, L 2000 *The Common Lands of England: A biological survey*. Aberystwyth: Univ of Wales Rural Surveys Res Unit

Allen, R 1997 'The battle for the common: Politics and populism in mid-Victorian Kentish London'. *Social Hist* **22** pt 1, 61–77

Alnmouth Common News **2**, Spring 1999

Altham, H S 1962 *A History of Cricket*, Vol 1. London: Allen & Unwin

Anon 1804a 'York August meeting'. *York Herald*, 25 August 1804, 3

Anon 1804b 'York August meeting concluded'. *York Herald*, 1 September 1804, 3

Anon 1902 *A Calendar to the Records of the Borough of Doncaster*, Vol 4. Doncaster: Corporation of Doncaster

Anon 1920 *Annual Report of the City Surveyor*. Lincoln: City of Lincoln

Archer, I 2000 'Politics and government 1540–1700' *in* Clark, P (ed) *The Cambridge Urban History of Britain*, Vol 2 (1540–1840). Cambridge: Cambridge University Press, 235–62

Astill, G G 1978 *Historic Towns in Berkshire: An archaeological appraisal*. Reading: Berkshire Archaeol Unit

Beresford, M W 1998 *History on the Ground* (rev edn). Stroud: Sutton

Birtles, S 1999 'Common land, poor relief and enclosure: The use of manorial resources in fulfilling parish obligations 1601–1834'. *Past and Present* **165**, 74–106

Borsay, P 1986 'The rise of the promenade: The social and cultural use of space in the English provincial town *c* 1660–1800'. *Brit J for Eighteenth-Century Stud* **9**, 125–40

Borsay, P 1989 *The English Urban Renaissance*. Oxford: Clarendon Press

Bourdillon, J 1988 'Countryside and town: The animal resources of Saxon Southampton' *in* Hooke, D (ed) *Anglo-Saxon Settlements*. Oxford: Blackwells, 177–95

Bowden, M C B, Ford, S and Mees, G with Gaffney, V 1993 'The date of the ancient fields on the Berkshire Downs'. *Berkshire Archaeol J* **74** (1991–3), 109–33

Bowers, J 1998 'Inter-war land drainage and policy in England and Wales'. *Agr Hist Rev* **46** pt 1, 64–80

Brian, A 1999 'The allocation of strips in Lammas Meadows by the casting of lots'. *Landscape Hist* **21**, 43–58

Broadbent, J F 1997 'Dewsbury inclosure 1796–1806'. *Yorkshire Archaeol J* **69**, 209–26

Brown, G 2003 *An Earthwork Survey and Investigation of Lincoln, West Common* (Archaeological Investigation Report Series AI/11/2003). Swindon: English Heritage

Brown, G and Field, D 2007 'Training trenches on Salisbury Plain: Archaeological evidence for battle training in the Great War'. *Wiltshire Archaeol Natur Hist Mag* **100**, 170–80

Browning, R 1955 *A History of Golf: The royal and ancient game*. London: Dent

Carter, H 1983 *An Introduction to Urban Historical Geography*. London: Edward Arnold

Castle, D, McCunnall, J and Tring, I 1984 *Field Drainage Principles and Practices*. London: Batsford

Charlton, D B and Day, J C 1977 *An Archaeological Survey of the Ministry of Defence Training Area, Otterburn, Northumberland* (unpublished report)

Charlton, R J 1933 *A History of Newcastle upon Tyne from the Earliest Records to its Formation as a City*. (First pub 1885). Newcastle: W H Robinson

Clark, J E 1990 'The battle for Mousehold Heath 1857–1884: "Popular politics" and the Victorian public park'. *Past and Present* **127**, 117–54

Clark, P 1984 'The civic leaders of Gloucester 1580–1800' *in* Clark, P (ed) *The Transformation of English Provincial Towns*. London: Hutchinson, 311–45

Clark, P and Slack, P 1976 *English Towns in Transition 1500–1700*. London: Oxford University Press

Clayden, P 2003 *Our Common Land: The law and history of commons and village greens*. Henley-on-Thames: Open Spaces Soc

Clifford, E M 1937 'The earthworks at Rodborough, Amberley and Minchinhampton, Gloucestershire'. *Trans Bristol Gloucestershire Archaeol Soc* **59**, 287–308

Connor, S E 2003 'A study of the urban commons of Oxfordshire: The survival of archaeological evidence for activity on the common lands of historic towns'. Unpublished MSt dissertation, Oxford University Dept of Continuing Education

Cook, H and Williamson, T 1999 *Water Management in the English Landscape: Field, marsh and meadow*. Edinburgh: Edinburgh University Press

Cowell, B 2002 'The Commons Preservation Society and the campaign for Berkhamsted Common, 1866–70'. *Rural Hist* **13**, 145–61

Crawford, O G S 1925 *Long Barrows of the Cotswolds*. Gloucester: John Bellows

Darby, H 1965 *The Draining of the Fens*. Cambridge: Cambridge University Press

Darvill, T 1998 'Landscapes, archaeology and the National Trust' *in* Jones, M and Rotherham, I (eds) *Landscapes, Perception, Recognition and Management*. Sheffield: Wildtrack, 9–18

Dyer, J 1963 'The Chiltern Grim's Ditch'. *Antiquity* **37**, 46–9

Elliott, P A 2000 'Derby Arboretum (1840): The first specially designed public park in Britain'. *Midland Hist* **26**, 144–76

Elliott, S 1972 'The open field system of an urban community: Stamford in the nineteenth century'. *Agr Hist Rev* **20** pt 2, 155–69

Elsworth, D W 2005a *Hoad, Ulverston, Cumbria: Archaeological landscape investigation* (privately produced report)

Elsworth, D W 2005b *Kendal Fell, Kendal, Cumbria: Conservation Plan (Draft)*. Lancaster: Oxford Archaeology North

English Heritage 2002 *With Alidade and Tape: Graphical and plane table survey of archaeological earthworks*. Swindon: English Heritage

English Heritage 2003 *Where on Earth Are We? The Global Positioning System (GPS) in archaeological field survey*. Swindon: English Heritage

English Heritage 2007a *Understanding the Archaeology of Landscapes: A guide to good recording practice*. Swindon: English Heritage

English Heritage 2007b *Golf in Historic Parks and Landscapes*. London: English Heritage

English Heritage 2008 *Climate Change and the Historic Environment*. London: Centre for Sustainable Heritage, University College London with English Heritage

Everitt, A 1974 'The Banburys of England'. *Urban Hist Yearb* **1**, 28–38

Everitt, A 2000 'Common land' in Thirsk, J (ed) *The English Rural Landscape*. Oxford: Oxford University Press, 210–35

Eversley, Lord 1910 *Commons, Forests and Footpaths: The story of the battle during the last forty-five years for public rights over commons, forests and footpaths of England and Wales*. London: Cassell

Everson, P L and Bowden, M C B 2002 'Wastes and Strays': The archaeology of urban commons (unpublished project proposal for HSLAC (EH Historic Landscapes Committee) 2002/2)

Field, D 1998 'Round barrows and the harmonious landscape: Placing early Bronze Age burial monuments in south-east England'. *Oxford J Archaeol* **17** no 3, 309–26

Field, D 2005 *South Common, Lincoln: An archaeological investigation of an urban open space* (Archaeological Investigation Report Series AI/18/2005). Swindon: English Heritage

Fletcher, M 2003 *Corfe Common, Purbeck, Dorset* (Archaeological Investigation Report Series AI/28/2003). Swindon: English Heritage

Francis, P 2002 'Okehampton Artillery Range, Devon: Report and photographic survey'. (Unpublished report for Defence Estates, Exeter)

The Freemen of the City of Newcastle upon Tyne, 'The Hoppings', *The Freemen of Newcastle upon Tyne* (2008), http://www.freemenofnewcastle. org/

French, H 2000 'Urban agriculture, commons and commoners in the seventeenth and eighteenth centuries: The case of Sudbury, Suffolk'. *Agr Hist Rev* **48** pt 2, 171–99

French, H 2003 'Urban common rights, enclosure and the market: Clitheroe Town Moors, 1764–1802'. *Agr Hist Rev* **51** pt 1, 40–68

Giles, P M 1950 'The enclosure of common lands in Stockport'. *Trans Lancashire Cheshire Antiq Soc* **62**, 73–110

Gillett, E A 1970 *History of Grimsby*. Oxford: Oxford University Press

Gillies, J 1837 *Memoirs of the Rev George Whitefield*. Middletown: Hunt & Noyes

Girouard, M 1990 *The English Town*. New Haven and London: Yale University Press

Glennie, P and Whyte, I 2000 'Towns in an agrarian economy 1540–1700' in Clark, P (ed) *The Cambridge Urban History of Britain*, Vol 2 (1540–1840). Cambridge: Cambridge University Press, 167–94

Goldthorpe, R 2006 *Clifton and Durdham Downs: A landscape history*. Bristol: Bristol City Council

Graham, D, Graham, A and Wiltshire, P 2004 'Investigation of a Bronze Age mound on Thursley Common'. *Surrey Archaeol Collect* **91**, 151–66

Hall, D 1981 'The origins of open-field agriculture – the archaeological fieldwork evidence' in Rowley, T (ed) *The Origins of Open-Field Agriculture*. London: Croom Helm, 22–38

Hammond, B 1931 'Two towns' enclosures'. *Econ Hist Rev* **2** (1930–3), 258–66

Hargrove, E 1809 *The History of the Castle, Town and Forest of Knaresborough with Harrogate*. Knaresborough: Hargrove and Sons

Haslam, J 1984 'The towns of Wiltshire' in Haslam, J (ed) *Anglo-Saxon Towns in Southern England*. Chichester: Phillimore, 87–148

Haythornthwaite, W 1959 'The Stray'. *Harrogate Advertiser* **1**, 29 Aug 1959

HERSG (Historic Environment Review Steering Group) 2000 *Power of Place: The future of the historic environment*. London: English Heritage

Hill, C 1991 *The World Turned Upside Down: Radical ideas during the English Revolution*. Harmondsworth: Penguin

Hodgetts, C 2003 *Worcester's Riverside Parks*. Worcester: Worcester City Council

Hodson, W W 1891 'John Colney's or St Leonard's Hospital for Lepers at Sudbury'. *Suffolk Inst Archaeol Natur Hist* **7**, 268–74

Hooke, D 1981 'Open-field agriculture – the evidence from pre-Conquest charters of the West Midlands' in Rowley, T (ed) *The Origins of Open-Field Agriculture*. London: Croom Helm, 39–63

Hoskins, W G 1988 *Making of the English Landscape*. (First pub 1955, rev edn with introduction and commentary by C C Taylor). London: Hodder & Stoughton

Hoskins, W G and Stamp, L D 1963 *The Common Lands of England and Wales*. London: Collins

Horsell Common Preservation Society, 'The sandpit', *Horsell Common Preservation Society*, www.horsellcommon.co.uk/sandpithc.htm

Hull, P (Godmanchester Community Association), *The Past of Portholme* (1999), www.godmanchester.net/history/portholme.htm

Humphries, J 1990 'Enclosures, common rights, and women: The proletarianization of families in the late eighteenth and early nineteenth centuries'. *J Econ Hist* **50**, 17–42

Hunter, R 1867 'The preservation of commons' in *Six Essays on Commons Preservation: Written in competition for prizes offered by Henry W Peek*. London: Sampson Low, Son and Marston, 307–75

Huntingdonshire Local History Society 1992 *Huntingdon: The aviation centre* (reprint of 1910 booklet). Huntingdon: Huntingdonshire Local History Soc

Hurley J, 2002 *Tom Spring, Bare-Knuckle Champion of All England*. Stroud: Tempus

Hutchins, J 1863 *The History and Antiquities of the County of Dorset*, Vol 2, 3 edn. Westminster: John Bowyer Nichols and Sons

Jones, M J, Stocker, D and Vince, A with Herridge, J 2003 *The City by the Pool: Assessing the archaeology of the City of Lincoln* (Lincoln Archaeol Studies **10**). Oxford: Oxbow

Jones, R 1998 *Unseen Worcester*. Worcester: Parkbarn

Kerridge, E 1992 *The Common Fields of England*. Manchester: Manchester University Press

Lambert, D and Williams, S 2005 *Commons, Heaths and Greens in Greater London: A short report for English Heritage*. London: The Parks Agency

Lambert, F 1921 'Some recent excavations in London'. *Archaeologia* **71**, 55–112

Lambrick, G and McDonald, A 1985 'The archaeology and ecology of Port Meadow and Wolvercote Common, Oxford' in Lambrick, G (ed) *Archaeology and Nature Conservation*. Oxford: Oxford University Department for External Studies, 95–109

Large, P 1984 'Urban growth and agricultural change in the West Midlands during the seventeenth and eighteenth centuries' in Clark, P (ed) *The Transformation of English Provincial Towns*. London: Hutchinson, 169–89

Laughton, J and Dyer, C 1999 'Small towns in the east and west midlands in the later Middle Ages: A comparison'. *Midland Hist* **24**, 24–52

Lewis, G H 1976 *Wings over the Somme 1916–18*. London: William Kimber

Lloyd, D 1992 *The Making of the English Town: 2000 years of evolution*. London: Gollancz

Lofthouse, C A 1995 *Town Moor, Newcastle* (unpublished archaeological survey report). Newcastle: RCHME

Mabey, R 2001 *Food for Free* (rev edn). London: Harper Collins

Maidlow, J 1867 'The law of commons and open spaces' in *Six Essays on Commons Preservation: Written in competition for prizes offered by Henry W Peek*. London: Sampson Low, Son and Marston, 1–81

Maitland, F W 1897 *Township and Borough: With an appendix of notes relating to the history of Cambridge* (reprinted 1964). Cambridge: Cambridge University Press

McDonald, A 2007 *The Historical Ecology of Some Unimproved Alluvial Grassland in the Upper Thames Valley* (Brit Archaeol Rep **441**). Oxford: Archaeopress

McOmish, D S 2005 'Bronze Age land allotment on the Marlborough Downs' in Brown, G, Field, D and McOmish, D S (eds) *The Avebury Landscape: Aspects of the field archaeology of the Marlborough Downs*. Oxford: Oxbow, 133–6

McOmish, D S, Field, D and Brown, G 2002 *The Field Archaeology of the Salisbury Plain Training Area*. Swindon: English Heritage

McOmish, D S and Newsome, S 2006 *Biggleswade Common, Biggleswade, Bedfordshire* (unpublished archaeological survey report). English Heritage

Mellor, H E 1976 *Leisure and the Changing City 1870–1914*. London: Routledge & Kegan Paul

Moore, J 1945 *Portrait of Elmbury*. London: Collins

Munby, J 1984 'Saxon Chichester and its predecessors' in Haslam, J (ed) *Anglo-Saxon Towns in Southern England*. Chichester: Phillimore, 315–30

National Fairground Archive, University of Sheffield, 'A few punches more: The fairground boxing show', *National Fairground Archive* (2007a), http://www.nfa.dept.shef.ac.uk/history/shows/boxing.html

National Fairground Archive, University of Sheffield, 'Buffalo Bill's Wild West', *National Fairground Archive* (2007b), http://www.nfa.dept.shef.ac.uk/history/shows/wildwest.html

Neeson, J M 1993 *Commoners: Common right, enclosure and social change in England, 1700–1820*. Cambridge: Cambridge University Press

Newcastle City Council 2004 *Local Studies Library Fact Sheet 3: Town Moor Hoppings*. Newcastle: Education & Libraries Directorate

Newsome, S 2005 *Hungerford Common, Freeman's Marsh and Environs* (EH Aerial Survey and Investigation Special Project AER/5/2005). Swindon: English Heritage

Page, F M 1993 *A History of Hertford*, 2 edn. Hertford: Hertford Town Council

Pain, O 1992 *Tewkesbury the Day Before Yesterday*. Leominster: Orpheus Press

Pearson, T 1996 *Lingheath Farm, Brandon, Suffolk* (unpublished archaeological survey report). Cambridge: RCHME

Pearson, T and Pollington, M 2004 *Westwood Common, Beverley: An archaeological survey* (Archaeological Investigation Report Series AI/25/2004). Swindon: English Heritage

Phillips, C B 1984 'Town and country: Economic change in Kendal, *c* 1550–1700' *in* Clark, P (ed) *The Transformation of English Provincial Towns*. London: Hutchinson, 99–132

Plastow, N 1986 'Military uses of the commons' *in* Plastow, N (ed) *A History of Wimbledon and Putney Commons*. London: Conservators of Wimbledon and Putney Commons, 27–32

Platt, C 1976 *The English Medieval Town*. London: Secker & Warburg

Pollington, M 2004 *Walmgate Stray, York: An archaeological survey* (Archaeological Investigation Report Series AI/36/2004). Swindon: English Heritage

Pollington, M and Pearson, T 2004 *Figham Common, Beverley: An archaeological survey* (Archaeological Investigation Report Series AI/23/2004). Swindon: English Heritage

Poole, S 1999 '"Till our liberties be secure": Popular sovereignty and public space in Bristol, 1750–1850'. *Urban Hist* **26**, 40–54

Poppy, S, Popescu, E and Drummond-Murray, J 2006 'Fieldwork in Cambridgeshire 2005'. *Proc Cambridge Antiq Soc* **95**, 183–9

Rackham, O 1986 *The History of the Countryside*. London: Dent

Rice, J 1879 *History of the British Turf from the Earliest Times to the Present Day*. London: Sampson Low, Marston, Searle and Rivington

Ruddock, J G 1983 *The Lincolnshire Agricultural Society*. Lincoln: Lincolnshire Agricultural Society

Russett, V 1991 *The Minchinhampton Commons, Gloucestershire: The National Trust Archaeological Survey*. Gloucester: Gloucestershire County Council

Schofield, J, Beck, C and Drollinger, H 2003 'The archaeology of opposition: Greenham Common and Peace Camp, Nevada'. *Conservation Bulletin* **44**, 47–9

Scurfield, G 1986 'Seventeenth-century Sheffield and its environs'. *Yorkshire Archaeol J* **58**, 147–71

Sheahan, J J and Whellan, T 1856 *The History and Topography of the City of York; The Ainsty Wapentake, and the East Riding of Yorkshire*, Vol 2. Beverley: John Green

Short, C 2000 'Common land and ELMS: A need for policy innovation in England and Wales'. *Land Use Policy* **17**, 121–33

Short, C Hayes, E, Selman, P and Wragg, A 2005 *A Common Purpose: A guide to agreeing management on common land*. Cheltenham: Countryside & Community Research Institute, University of Gloucestershire

Short, C and Winter, M 1999 'The problem of common land: Towards stakeholder governance'. *J Environmental Planning & Management* **42** (5), 613–30

Smith, E 2004 *Hob Moor Historic Stray and Local Nature Reserve*. York: William Sessions

Smith, G 2005 'Old English *leah* and Surrey's rough grazing commons'. *Bull Surrey Archaeol Soc* **385**, 7–10

Smith, N A 2002 *Minchinhampton Common: An archaeological survey of the earthwork remains* (Archaeological Investigation Report Series AI/12/2002). Swindon: English Heritage

Southampton City Council 2007 *Southampton Common Green Flag Management Plan 2007–2010*. Southampton

Swallow, S C 1999 *The Defence of Lincolnshire 1793–1802*. Lincolnshire Archives (self-published)

Swallow, S C 2000 *The Defence of Lincolnshire 1803–1815*. Lincolnshire Archives (self-published)

Tavener, L E 1957 *The Common Lands of Hampshire*. London: Hampshire County Council

Taylor, C C 1999 'Post-medieval drainage of marsh and fen' *in* Cook, H and Williamson, T (eds) *Water Management in the English Landscape: Field, marsh and meadow*. Edinburgh: Edinburgh University Press, 141–56

Thirsk, J 1984 *The Rural Economy of England: Collected essays*. London: The Hambledon Press

Thomas, R M 2006 'Mapping the towns: English Heritage's Urban Survey and Characterization Programme'. *Landscapes* **7** pt 1, 68–92

Thompson, E P 1991 *Customs in Common*. London: Merlin Press

Thompson, I and Bryant, S 2005 *Berkhamsted*. Hertfordshire County Council Historic Environment Unit Extensive Urban Surveys (revised assessment)

VCH Ches V 2005 *A History of the County of Chester: The City of Chester, Vol V* (Pt 2). Woodbridge: Boydell & Brewer

VCH Essex IX 1994 *A History of the County of Essex: The Borough of Colchester, Vol IX*. Oxford: Oxford University Press

VCH Glos VIII 1968 *A History of the County of Gloucester, Vol VIII*. London: Oxford University Press

VCH Herts III 1912 *The Victoria History of the County of Hertford, Vol III*. London: Archibald Constable

VCH Hunts II 1932 *The Victoria History of the County of Huntingdon, Vol II*. London: St Catherine Press

VCH Lancs III 1907 *The Victoria History of the County of Lancaster, Vol III*. London: Archibald Constable

VCH Lancs VI 1911 *The Victoria History of the County of Lancaster, Vol VI*. London: Constable

VCH Northants III 1930 *The Victoria History of the County of Northampton, Vol III*. London: St Catherine Press

VCH Staffs II 1967 *A History of the County of Stafford, Vol II*. London: Oxford University Press

VCH Staffs VI 1979 *A History of the County of Stafford, Vol VI*. Oxford: Oxford University Press

VCH Wilts VIII 1965 *A History of Wiltshire, Vol VIII*. London: Oxford University Press

VCH Wilts XII 1983 *A History of Wiltshire, Vol XII*. Oxford: Oxford University Press

VCH Worcs III 1913 *The Victoria History of the County of Worcester, Vol III*. London: Constable

VCH York 1961 *A History of Yorkshire: The City of York*. London: Oxford University Press

VCH Yorks VI 1989 *A History of the County of York: East Riding, Vol VI*. Oxford: Oxford University Press

Vincent, W T 1888 *The Records of the Woolwich District, Vol 2*. Woolwich: J P Jackson

Wager, S J 1998 *Woods, Wolds and Groves: The woodland of medieval Warwickshire* (Brit Archaeol Rep **269**). Oxford: J & E Hedges

Walford, E 1878 *Old and New London, Vol 6*. London: Cassell, Peter & Galpin

Walker, A 2004 'The Lincolnshire Show, 1869–1913: Rural and urban encounters on the showground' *in* Mansfield, N, Sheeran, G, Stokes, W, Tebbutt, M and Walton, J (eds) *Rural and Urban Encounters in the Nineteenth and Twentieth Centuries: Regional perspectives*. Conference of Regional and Local Historians, 41–57

Walker, H H nd *The History of Harrogate Stray* (privately printed)

Walls, J and Parker, C 2000 *Aircraft Made in Lincoln*. Lincoln: Society for Lincolnshire History and Archaeology

Warner, P 1987 *Greens, Commons and Clayland Colonization: The origins and development of greenside settlement in east Suffolk* (Department of English Local History Occasional Papers ser 4, no **2**). Leicester: Leicester University Press

Watson, S 1960 *The Reign of George III 1760–1815* (The Oxford History of England **12**). Oxford: Clarendon Press

Welfare, H G and Swan, V G 1995 *Roman Camps in England: The field archaeology*. London: HMSO

Wesley, C 1909 *The Journal of Charles Wesley: The early journal 1736–1739*. London: Robert Culley

Whitefield, G 1965 *Whitefield's Journals*. London: The Banner of Truth Trust

Willis, S 2007 'Roman towns, Roman landscapes: The cultural terrain of town and country in the Roman period' *in* Fleming, A and Hingley, R (eds) *Prehistoric and Roman Landscapes* (Landscape History after Hoskins, Vol 1). Macclesfield: Windgather Press, 143–64

Willmott Dobbie, B M 1979 *Pounds or Pinfolds, and Lockups*. Bath: University of Bath

Woodward, L 1962 *The Age of Reform 1815–1870* (The Oxford History of England **13**). Oxford: Clarendon Press

York Herald, 20 June 1928, 1 (advertisement for York Gala and Flower Show)

Figures in **bold** refer to illustrations.

A

Abingdon Common 47, 52
aerial photography 12, 80
  use of aerial photographs 14,
    15, 21, 48, 51, 52, 56, 81
agricultural shows 32, 56, **61**,
  61–2
Aircraft Acceptance Parks 51
airfields 50, **50**, 51, 54
Albert, Prince 45
allotments 21, 57
Alnmouth Common 25
anti-glider and anti-tank obstacles
  50, 52
'Anti-mill', *see* Beverley
aqueduct 41, **41**, **42**
arable land 1, 2, 7, 21, 22, **22**, 23,
  32
arboretums 58–60, **59**
archaeological survey 81–2
archery practice 44, 45–6, **46**
artesian well 42–3
assault course (Second World
  War) 50
assemblies 56
Assembly Green, Brightside,
    see Sheffield
Atherstone 10
athletics 61, 72
Atkinson, R J C 12
aviation
  civil 75
  military 50–1

B

Baildon Bank and Moor,
    see Bradford
ball games 7, 32, 64
  see also bowls; cricket; football;
    golf; tennis
Bampton 52
'Bandy' 66
Banstead Heath, *see* Reigate
Barnwell Priory, Cambridge 75
barracks 45, 55, 57, 62
barrows 11–12

Bronze Age **2**, 11–12, 14, 19, 46,
  65
  Iron Age 12, **12**
  Neolithic 11, **11**
Bath 58
bathing 65–6
Beaminster Down 46
  Beaminster Butts 46
bear-baiting 7, 64
beast gates, *see* cattle gates
bell-pits 36, 37, **37**
Berkhamsted 6, 9
  Common 10, 13, 14, 15, 38, 45,
    45
Bevan, Mary Ann 68
Beverley 11, 12, 24, 32, 34
  Figham Common 24, 25, 28–30,
    31, 38, 39, 47, 52
  Beverley and Barmston Drain
    30
  Beverley and Skidby Drain 30
  Hurn Common 24, 62
  Swine Moor 25, 28, 30, 38, 39,
    61
  New Main Drain 30
  Swinemoor Wells 61
  Westwood Common 14, 21, 24,
    25, 31, 62, **80**
  airfield 51
  'Anti-mill' and Black Mill 40,
    41
  bull-baiting 64, **65**
  enclosure 15–16, **17**
  military activity 48, **49**
  prehistoric remains 12, **12**
  quarries and limekiln 34, 35,
    36
  recreation 57, 65
  windmills 40, **41**, **49**
  woodland 38, 39
Biggleswade 11, 81
  Common 14–15, 30, 37, 43, **51**,
    52, **81**
Big Meadow, *see* Loughborough
billets 46
Biodiversity Action Plans 76
Blackheath Common, *see* London
Black Mill, *see* Beverley
Bolton 8
bonfires 32, **56**, 68
Bootham Stray, *see* York
Borough Fen, *see* Peterborough
boundaries, common

medieval and later 30–1
  Roman 18
Bournemouth 19, 58
bowls 65
boxing 70, **70**, 75
bracken 1, 38
Bradford 58
  Baildon Bank and Moor 40
Brandon 6, 17
Brandon Hill, *see* Bristol
brick-making 34, 38
Bridlington 46
Brighton 2, 19, 80
brine baths 43
Bristol 6, 30, 32, 40, 76
  Brandon Hill 8, 40, 63, 73, 74, **74**
  Cabot Tower 74
  Clifton Down 32, 35
  Downs 30
  Durdham Down 30, **30**, 32, 35,
    43, 72
Buffalo Bill's Wild West Show 32,
  68
building materials 33
bull-baiting 64, **65**
bulrushes 39
Burford, High Mead 27
burgage properties 3, 12, 23
burgesses 3, 8, 18, 23, 24, 38, 39,
  55
burial mounds, *see* barrows
Buriton 19
'bush drains' 30
Butt Hill, Bridlington 46
butts
  archery 45, 46
  rifle **16**, 47–8

C

Cabot, John 74
Calne 24
Camberwell New Road 37
Cambridge 2
  Donkey's Common 62
  Laundress Green **ii**
  Midsummer Common 68, **68**,
    74–5
  Port Field (Carme Field) 18
  Scholars' Piece **10**
camps
  military 44, 50, 51, 52, 54, 55

'peace camp' 54
  Roman 15, **15**
canals 37
Canford Heath, *see* Poole
Canwick Park 15
car boot sales 75
Carme Field, *see* Cambridge
carnival **67**
Castle Leazes, *see* Newcastle upon
    Tyne
cattle 6, 10, **10**, 20, 23, 24, 25,
  26, **26**, 27, 32, 37, 57, **64**
cattle gates 24, 32
cattle market 58
cavalry training 47
celebrations 45, 56, 58, 67, 74–5,
  76
cemeteries
  medieval and later 3, 8, 57, 62,
    63
  Roman 15
Chadwell Spring, Hertford **41**
Chapel Fields, *see* Norwich
Charles II 50
Chartists 74
Chelmsford 19
  Galleywood Common 72
Chelsea Common, *see* London
Chesham 6
Chester, The Roodee 19
Chichester
  common 8
  Portfield 18
Chiltern Grim's Ditch 13–14, 15
Chiltern Hills 23, 38
Chippenham, West Mead 27
circuses 68, 75, 76, **78**
civil unrest 6, 9, 73, 74, **74**, 76
Clapham Common, *see* London
Clare, Richard de, Earl of
    Gloucester 5, 18
classic car rallies 75
clay 34, 35
clay pits 34, 66
Clayton, Tommy 25
Clifton Down, *see* Bristol
climate change 76, 82
Clitheroe 3, 6, 32
  Town Moors 24, 72
clothes drying 1, **40**, 46
coal 8, 34, 36–7, 39
Coalville 19
Cobham, Sir Alan 75